BLOCKCHAIN, BITCOIN AND BEYOND

Beginner-Friendly Bite-Sized Chunks

AF869865

AJINKYA LATKAR

notionpress.com

INDIA • SINGAPORE • MALAYSIA

ISBN 979-8-89363-873-8

Dedicated to 3 highly academic and inspiring
ladies in my life – My mother Dr. Madhuwanti Latkar,
my sister Tejasi Latkar, and my wife
Vyshnavi Garimella Latkar.

CONTENTS

Cryptocurrencies

Web3

Technical Challenges and Solutions

Economics, Security, and Regulation

New Frontiers and Future Outlook

WHY THIS BOOK?

Blockchain technology has sparked a remarkable revolution over the past decade and a half, primarily through the advent of cryptocurrencies but also through its other diverse applications in a variety of industries. Beginning as a niche topic of interest in 2008 (through Bitcoin's whitepaper), it has since become an inescapable part of the modern digital landscape. In fact, more likely than not, you would already have crossed paths with it – directly or indirectly, knowingly or unknowingly – at some point in the last 15 years.

I first took a serious look at it in 2017, when I was part of a team developing an internet of things (IoT) diagnostics toolkit for consulting gigs in manufacturing industries. At some point during that, a co-worker said, and I quote, "...ensuring no one tampers with the vast amounts of data collected is difficult, I wonder if we could use something like a blockchain...", and then proceeded to follow that up with a very funky-sounding monologue on blockchain technology that made me feel like I'd been living under a rock. So, with a bout of curiosity (peppered with a fear of missing out), I turned to the internet hoping to find a quick rundown on it, but instead was plunged into an unending series of rabbit-holes.

Although we ended up not using blockchain for our IoT diagnostics toolkit, it became a regular hobby for me from that point on. Bit by bit, the non-fiction section of my bookshelf piled up with books on blockchain technology. I started spending significant amounts of my free time on forums, learning about the latest and greatest of this world. I read whitepapers of blockchain projects like thriller novels. I even learnt to code in Solidity, to be able to read and write smart contracts.

From Bitcoin's inception to the most bizarre-sounding cryptocurrencies, from smart contracts to decentralized applications, from the new era of the internet (Web3) to the evolving regulations around it – this world is truly fascinating. And although I don't claim to be an expert in it, I can confidently say that I have dabbled enough to have a sound understanding of its basic workings.

I decided to document my understanding in this book, because I believe that there is a general lack of easily digestible literature that can bring any reader, regardless of their technical background or appetite, up to speed with the subject. Most books/papers available are too technical or too focused on narrow aspects of the subject matter, and the internet is disorganized and often dominated by opinions more than facts.

This book is my attempt to help anyone who wishes to quickly understand how blockchain technology works, and what impact it has had in the world. It's a simple-worded starter pack covering the

essentials without getting claustrophobically deep into any concept.

Having said that, if you aspire to make a career in blockchain technology or want to gain deep and intuitive expertise in it, this book will only serve as a starting point, and you'll need to augment it with the next level of advanced and tactical know-how which is beyond its scope. For instance, this book will tell you what 'sharding' is and how it solves blockchain scalability issues, but it won't teach you how to implement a shard in a blockchain.

Last but not the least, a couple of important disclaimers. One, nothing in this book is any kind of financial or investment advice. If you are looking to profit from trading or investing in cryptocurrencies, this book won't help. And two, I neither represent nor endorse any specific cryptocurrency, blockchain, individual, organization, or technology named in this book.

Go ahead, then. Dive right in!

Happy trails!

– Ajinkya Latkar
March 2024

BLOCKCHAIN FUNDAMENTALS

1.

LET'S TALK BLOCKCHAIN

The words 'blockchain' and 'cryptocurrency' are often subconsciously entangled – in the sense, the mere mention of blockchain takes the brain straight to cryptocurrencies. First and foremost, let's set this record straight – blockchain is a versatile technology that has a variety of applications. Cryptocurrencies just happen to be the first and (as of now) the most extensive one of these applications. So, although cryptocurrencies will take up a large part of this book, don't let that cloud your understanding of blockchain technology's broad relevance.

At its core, blockchain technology provides a secure, transparent, and immutable (un-alterable) means of storing data digitally in structures called 'blockchains'.

The type of data stored on a blockchain is determined by its specific application. For instance, a blockchain running a cryptocurrency acts as a ledger storing transaction logs and account balances of the cryptocurrency. A blockchain used for supply chain management records the journey of products from source to consumer, capturing details like origin, shipment dates, and quality checks. Blockchain technology's data handling capabilities have evolved over time and can now manage a wide variety of data types and formats, thus broadening its applications across various industries.

A blockchain operates as an ecosystem where relevant data is continuously gathered, verified, and permanently stored. One of the core features of this ecosystem is 'decentralization'. Instead of a single authority, responsibility to curate data on a blockchain belongs to a vast network of 'nodes'. These nodes are bound by rules defined in the blockchain's 'consensus mechanism', which governs how data gets added to it. Data added to the blockchain is locked 'cryptographically', preventing any alterations or deletions.

I know, that was quite a lot of technical jargon packed into one paragraph, and we'll get to all the details in the next few chapters. For now, think of a blockchain as a jigsaw puzzle where anyone can insert pieces at the right places, but once inserted, the pieces are super-glued in place, and no one can remove or rearrange them.

So why the name 'blockchain'? It's because the word literally describes what the structure looks like. Verified data is permanently sealed into 'blocks', which are connected to each other in an ordered 'chain', which keeps getting longer with time. Ok, so a jigsaw puzzle is not really the best analogy, unless all the pieces only fit in a single row.

Blockchain technology was pioneered in 2008 by an individual (or it might have been a group of people) using the pseudonym Satoshi Nakamoto. It was initially conceptualized and designed to serve as the public transaction ledger for Bitcoin, the first cryptocurrency. The first ever blockchain was implemented in 2009 as part of the Bitcoin protocol. Since then, the technology has evolved far beyond Bitcoin to support a myriad of other cryptocurrencies and several other applications.

The Bitcoin blockchain was followed by other prominent blockchains like Ethereum, Cardano and Solana, which introduced features like versatile smart contracts, high speeds and efficient consensus mechanisms that the Bitcoin blockchain was missing. These features paved the way for numerous other applications beyond cryptocurrencies, such as supply chain management, healthcare, financial services, and more.

It's clear that blockchain is more than just a passing technological fad. It's a paradigm shift in our perspective on storing and accessing data, and it's here for the long run.

2.

DECENTRALIZATION: BLOCKCHAIN TECHNOLOGY'S CORE PREMISE

Imagine you are in a class with 100 students, where no one's really paying any attention to the instructor except that one guy sitting in the front row and taking notes feverishly. A night before the final examination, everyone photocopies this guy's notes in a desperate attempt to cram everything in record-breaking time (nostalgic yet?). But it turns out, our front row guy is malicious, so he changes his notes before anyone can photocopy them, so only he has the correct ones. The result – he's the only one who passes.

Next year, everyone realizes that they can't rely on one person's notes and risk failure. So, they all start taking notes, and compare them at the end of every class. If anyone makes a mistake in their notes, maliciously or otherwise, the others correct it. This way, everyone ends up with correct notes and passes all the examinations.

That's **decentralization – taking control from a single authority and distributing it to the masses.**

Decentralization has always existed in nature in several shapes and forms. Take the vast expanse of our universe, for example. No single galaxy in the universe decides how all of them move in the grand scheme of things, rather, they all influence each other through gravity. Back on Earth, have you ever seen a school of fish? It doesn't have a leader, rather each fish responds to its neighbors, which collectively maintains the group's formation.

Decentralization is the core premise of blockchain technology. Responsibility to curate data on a blockchain lies with a vast network of 'nodes' instead of a central authority.

Nodes of a blockchain are computers that actively manage data in its ecosystem, which requires running specific software and sometimes meeting certain hardware and connectivity standards. People or organizations who own these computers are called 'node operators', although they are sometimes informally called 'nodes' themselves.

Simply interacting with a blockchain, such as reading data stored on it or making transactions on it, does not make someone a node operator, they need to be running the blockchain's software to be classified as one. For public blockchains, the software is open source (available on the internet for free), and pretty much anyone with the required hardware and connectivity can become a node operator. For private, hybrid, and consortium blockchains, that privilege is often more selective.

Nodes in a blockchain's ecosystem work in tandem to verify incoming data, add it to the blockchain in new blocks, and validate these new blocks. Further, each node has a latest copy of the entire blockchain, ensuring its accuracy and security. This overall setup has 5 broad advantages.

It ensures that there's no single point of failure in the blockchain. If one or a few nodes face blackout, it doesn't derail the entire system since other nodes have their copies of the blockchain. This robustness is a stark contrast to centralized systems where malfunctions can grind them to a halt.

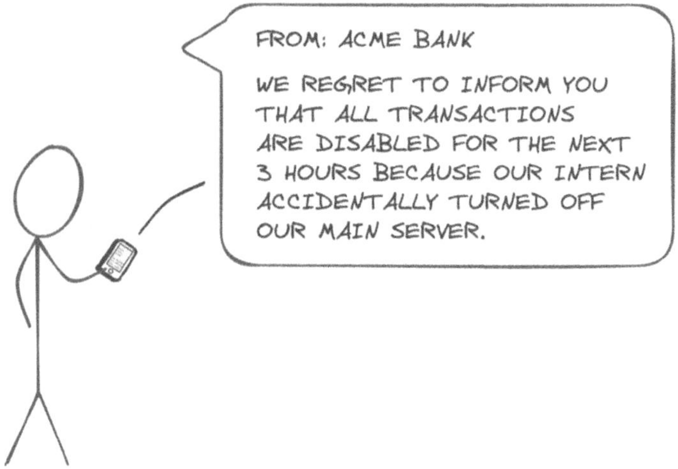

1. It imbues a sense of democratic decision making in the blockchain's ecosystem. New data can only be added to the blockchain strictly following its rules that are agreed upon by everyone in the ecosystem (node operators or otherwise). This ensures that multiple checks and balances are in place, and that no singular authority can control or manipulate data.
2. It ensures no one has an advantage through early availability or preferential access to data. All data added to a blockchain is openly accessible to all users in real-time, and no

authority can censor, abridge, or adulterate the data to their advantage, because once it's on the blockchain, it's unchangeable.

3. It makes the system very resistant to data losses or manipulations, because multiple copies of the blockchain are available across the network. If one node operator decides to tamper with their copy, the rest of them will disagree (because it won't match with their copies) and reject the tampered copy.
4. It makes processes cheaper and operationally efficient, since there are no authorities or intermediaries likely to cause delays for bureaucratic or selfish reasons.

Decentralization is a philosophical shift that moves power from centralized entities like governments, and places it in the hands of the wider community. This loss of power is one of the reasons why you see governments scrambling to either outright ban or create regulatory frameworks around blockchain technology and cryptocurrencies. Of course, there are other reasons like security and economic stability, which we'll discuss further ahead in the book.

3.

TYPES OF BLOCKCHAINS: PUBLIC, PRIVATE, AND MORE

Decentralization in blockchain technology promotes transparency, which means easy availability of data on blockchains to everyone. There are exceptions though, since complete transparency is not always feasible for all applications as it could compromise privacy. For instance, most people would prefer to keep their identity documents and medical records confidential.

From this point of view, broadly there are four types of blockchains: public, private, hybrid, and consortium. While public blockchains are entirely transparent, the other types address applications that require more discretion.

A public blockchain is like the open ocean – anyone can read its contents, setup nodes in its network, and otherwise contribute by developing and using applications on it. Bitcoin, Ethereum, Cardano, and Solana are examples of public blockchains.

While the openness of public blockchains offers a space for innovation and collective participation, it also makes them susceptible to all kinds of malicious activity such as scams and hacks. The level of transparency in public blockchains is also not suitable for types of data requiring a high degree of privacy and security.

A private blockchain, on the other hand, is like an aquarium – where privileges of reading data, setting up nodes, and developing applications are only available to a select few 'fish' with permissions. For this reason, private blockchains are also known as 'permissioned' blockchains. An example of such a blockchain is Quorum, developed by J.P. Morgan as an enterprise-focused version of Ethereum for use cases within the financial sector.

Even internally, private blockchains are usually controlled environments, in the sense even for users with permissions, access is not unrestricted within the blockchain, it is specific to individual permissions. These robust mechanisms make private blockchains more suitable for applications where a high degree of privacy and security is required, such as patient data management in healthcare. Private blockchains are also more protected from malicious attacks than public blockchains.

However, the restricted and centralized nature of private blockchains may raise concerns about trust and autonomy. After all, if only a few hold the keys, how can everyone be assured of fairness and impartiality?

With there being obvious merits and demerits of both public and private blockchains, there are hybrid blockchains that try to make the best of both worlds. These blockchains offer selective transparency, giving organizations the control to choose what privileges are open to the public, and what are not. Such a model aims to balance the transparency of public blockchains with the security of private ones. For instance, Dragonchain, originally developed at Disney's Seattle office, is a hybrid blockchain platform that enables businesses to selectively make transaction data public while keeping sensitive business information private.

Consortium blockchains, which can be classified as hybrid blockchains in a way, are controlled by a group instead of a single organization. In these blockchains, multiple entities make decisions in the best interest of the network. This multi-entity collaboration and control can offer better security and performance (e.g., higher transaction speeds) than public blockchains, and a more decentralized environment than private blockchains. Ripple, a platform optimized for fast cross-border money transfers, operates on a form of consortium blockchain.

4.

CRYPTOGRAPHY AND HOW DATA IS ADDED TO BLOCKCHAINS

Cryptography is the science of secure data storage and communication. It involves digitally obscuring data to ensure its confidentiality, integrity, authenticity, and sometimes anonymity, thereby preventing unauthorized access or tampering.

Cryptography is the cornerstone of modern digital security. It safeguards practically all data involved in your online interactions. For instance, it safeguards your email account, preventing unauthorized access to your personal inbox. It also ensures that when you send an email to someone, it is securely delivered exclusively to their inbox.

Blockchain technology leverages cryptography for ensuring data authenticity and immutability. While we won't delve much into the technical details of cryptography itself, we'll cover the essence of how it's used in most blockchains through a simplified example of a cryptocurrency transaction, showing how data is verified and permanently added to a blockchain. But first, it's important to understand two relevant cryptographic concepts: hash functions and public-key cryptography.

Hash functions

A 'hash function' is an algorithm that turns any given input into a seemingly random fixed-length binary output. This process is called 'hashing'. The output, referred to as the input's 'hash', is meant to be a unique representation, like a fingerprint, of the input.

A good hash function has the following properties –

- The inputs to the function can be of any length, but the output hashes always have a fixed length. E.g., the SHA-256 hash function used by the Bitcoin blockchain always produces 256-digit binary numbers as output hashes.

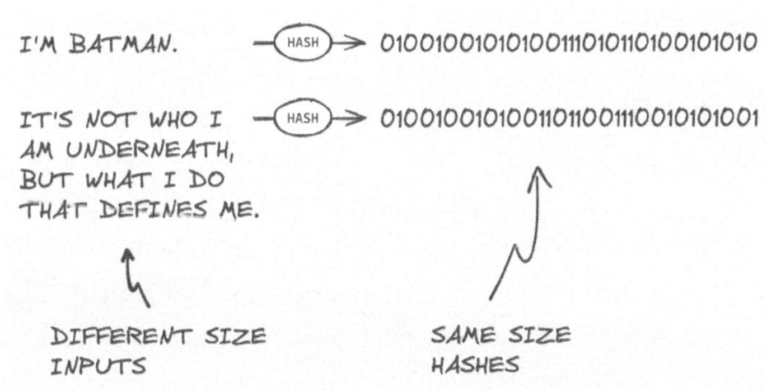

- Hashes appear random, in the sense, there is no discernible pattern between an input and its hash.

- Identical inputs to the function always produce the same hash.

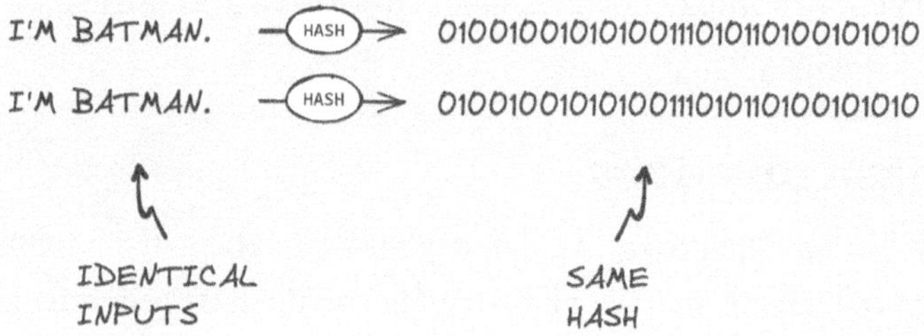

- With even a minor change in the input, the function produces a dramatically different hash that looks entirely unrelated to the previous one.

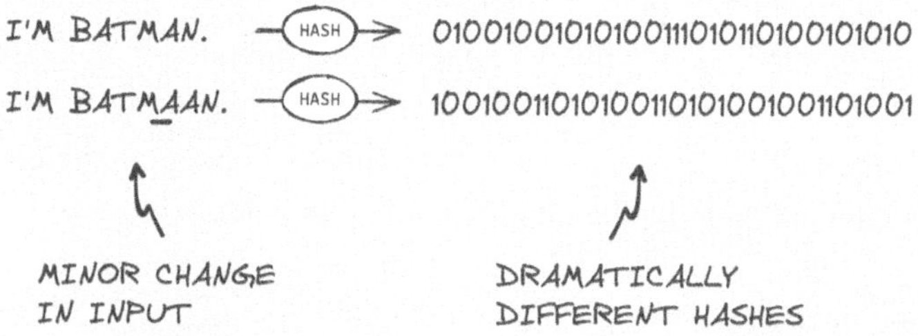

- Hashing is an irreversible process. Given an input, it's easy to compute its hash – just run it through the hash function. But given a hash, there is no direct way of determining its input – there is no 'reverse hash' function. The only way to do this, is with guesswork (i.e., guessing the input, running it through the hash function, and checking if its hash is the given one).

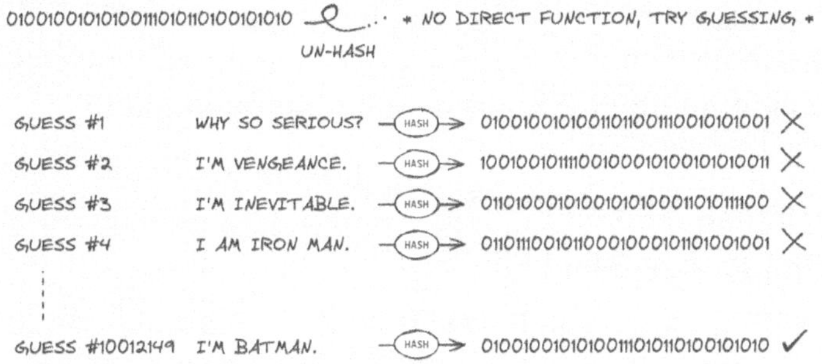

Please note that since hashing is irreversible, it does not qualify as 'encryption'. Encryption, by definition, is reversible, which means it's a process that obscures data in a way that allows its direct recovery through a corresponding 'decryption' process.

- Since the output length is fixed but the input length has no restriction, there are a limited number of outputs (hashes) possible for an infinite number of inputs. So, it is technically possible to guess multiple different inputs with the same given hash. But this is probabilistically extremely unlikely for hash functions like SHA-256, where the total number of possible hashes is 2^{256} which is a very, very large number. This property of hash functions is called 'collision resistance'.

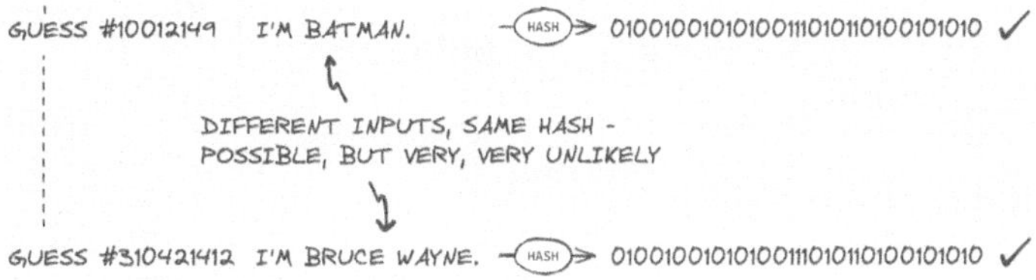

In blockchains, each block is uniquely identified by a hash which is generated by the blockchain's specific hash function using the data in the block as input.

Public-key cryptography

'Public-key cryptography', also called 'asymmetric cryptography', deploys a system of paired digital keys for encryption (scrambling) and decryption (un-scrambling) of data. Digital keys are binary numbers at their core, and each user of such a system owns a pair of them: a public key (openly accessible by everyone in the system) and a private key (kept secret by the owner).

The system works in the following way –

- Data encrypted with one key can only be decrypted with its paired key. For instance, if the private key encrypts data, only its paired public key can decrypt it, and vice versa.

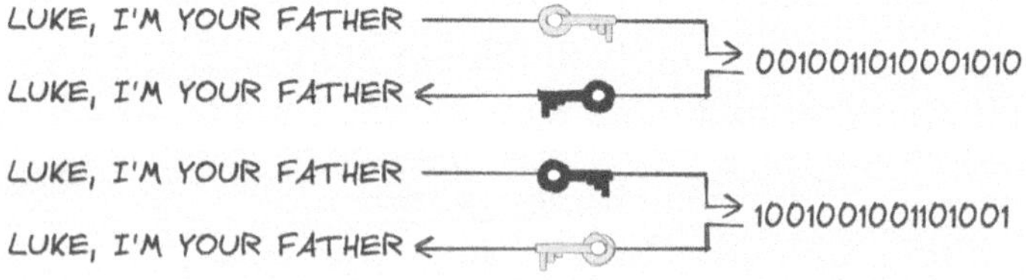

- If you try decryption with anything other than the paired key of the one that was used for encryption, you won't be able to get back the original data, instead you'll get garbage.
- Even a key itself cannot decrypt the data it encrypted, only its paired key can do that.

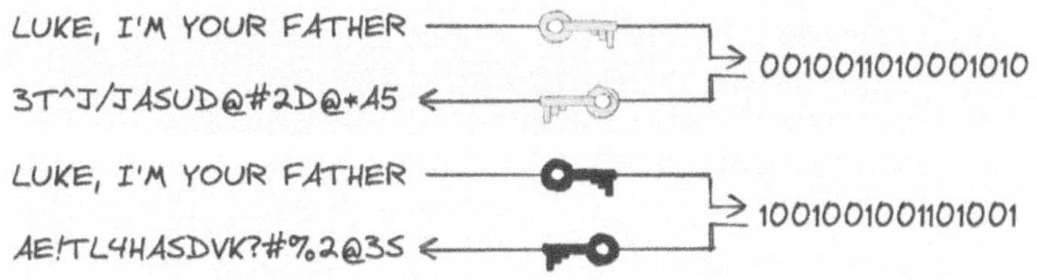

- Any small change in the input data dramatically changes its encryption, so that it looks completely different from the original data's encryption.

Blockchains use public-key cryptography for verifying data that is added to blockchains. At their core, public/private keys and encryptions are all binary numbers consisting of 0s and 1s. However, in the context of blockchains, they are often represented in other compact or human-readable formats, such as hexadecimals and mnemonic 12-24 word 'seed phrases', which we will cover in chapter 13.

Ok, so with hash functions and public-key cryptography under our belt, let's consider the following situation: Alice wants to send Bob 10 coins of a certain cryptocurrency.

Don't worry about fully understanding cryptocurrencies and how they work, we'll get to that further ahead in the book. For now, just keep in mind that a blockchain running a cryptocurrency acts as a ledger recording all transactions and balances of the cryptocurrency. Which means, the transaction between Alice and Bob will be completed when the corresponding blockchain adds it and updates their balances. Let's see how this happens, in 6 simplified steps.

Step 1: Alice creates a message "Alice is sending 10 coins to Bob" to initiate the transaction. The real message is more nuanced and includes elements such as Alice's and Bob's blockchain account 'addresses', a transaction fee (or 'gas fee'), and a unique transaction number – we'll cover these concepts further ahead in the book. For the sake of this example, let's go with the simplified message "Alice is sending 10 coins to Bob".

Alice then derives the hash of this message using the specific hash function of the blockchain protocol. This hash, as you know, is like a unique fingerprint for the message.

Step 2: Alice uses her private key to encrypt this hash. The result is called a 'digital signature'. This serves as proof that Alice is the genuine sender of the message, since only she possesses her unique private key.

Step 3: The transaction – which includes the original message ("Alice is sending 10 coins to Bob") and the digital signature – is then broadcast to the blockchain's network of nodes along with Alice's public key.

Each participating node in the network maintains a pool of unverified transactions, called a 'mempool'. Transactions that are broadcast to the network (like Alice's) are received by each node's mempool and remain there till they are verified and added to the blockchain.

Step 4: Participating nodes choose multiple unverified transactions from their mempools with the intention of verifying them and adding them to the blockchain.

Once Alice's transaction is picked up by a node, it first reads the original message and checks if Alice's blockchain account has equal to or more than 10 coins in it. If not, the transaction is rejected right away, since she cannot be sending 10 coins to Bob if she doesn't have them.

Once the node confirms that Alice has the required coin balance, it generates a hash for the original message ("Alice is sending 10 coins to Bob") using the same specific hash function of the blockchain protocol that Alice used – let's call this hash 'A'. Then, it uses Alice's public key to decrypt the digital signature and retrieve the hash which Alice initially generated for the message in step 1 – let's call this hash 'B'.

If A matches B, it verifies that Alice indeed initiated the transaction, and that the message along with the digital signature hasn't been intercepted and tampered on its way from Alice to the node's mempool.

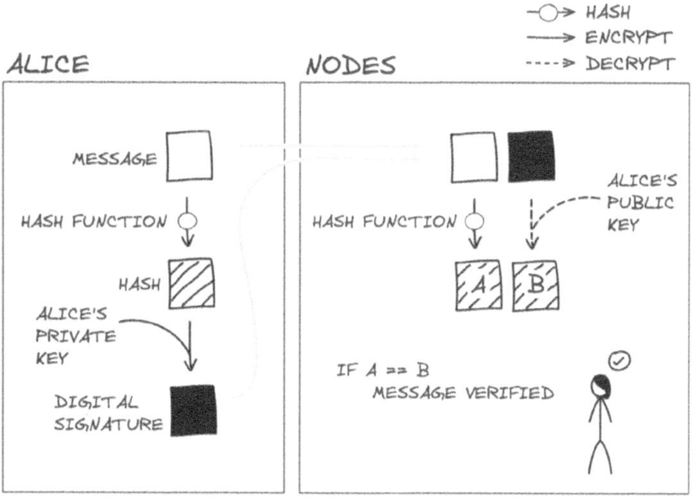

This cryptographic verification process of the transaction message is important because it ensures that only Alice has access to her blockchain account (through her private key). No impostor can broadcast messages pretending to be Alice, because if they try to do so, the verification will ultimately fail since they don't have Alice's private key to create her digital signatures.

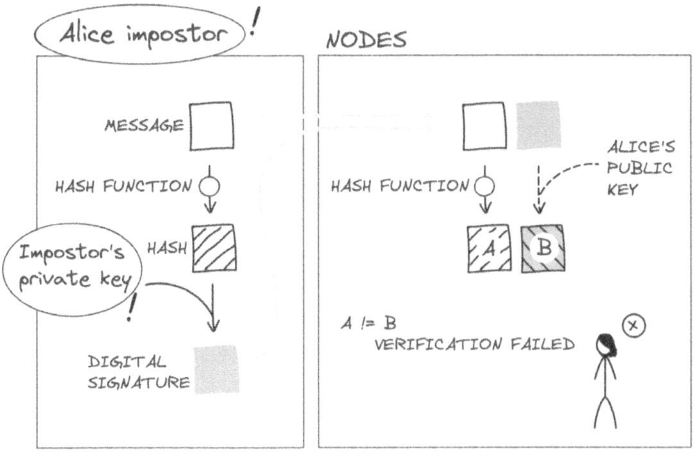

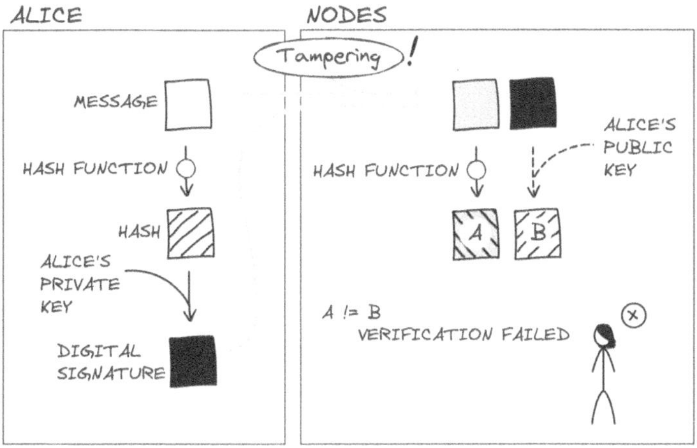

The verification process also ensures that there is no interference or tampering by anyone to change what Alice intends to do (in this case, send 10 coins to Bob). Any malicious actors intercepting the transaction before it reaches the mempool will only be able to tamper with the original message but not the accompanying digital signature (since they won't have access to Alice's private key). If they do make even a minor change to the original message alone, say from "Alice is sending 10 coins to Bob" to "Alice is sending 20 coins to Bob" or "Alice is sending 10 coins to Claire", the hashes of these two messages will be different, so A won't be the same as B, and the verification will fail.

Step 5: Once a node verifies all the transactions which it chose from its mempool (including Alice's), it starts the process of adding them to the blockchain.

The list of freshly verified transactions comprises of a new 'block'. To this block, the node adds the last validated block's hash from its latest copy of the blockchain. This is important to create a secure link between the two blocks (it's called a block"chain", remember?).

The node then finds a hash for the data in this new block following certain requirements. These requirements, and the exact way in which steps 4-5 are carried out in the ecosystem, are defined in the blockchain's 'consensus mechanism'. For instance, in 'Proof of Work' (PoW) blockchains, these steps are done in parallel by multiple participating nodes racing against each other, whereas in 'Proof of Stake' (PoS) blockchains, only one participating node is selected to perform these steps at a time. We will cover these consensus mechanisms in detail in the next chapter.

Step 6: When a hash meeting the requirements is found, the new block along with this hash is submitted to the network for validation. Other nodes in the network receive the new block and independently check it for sanctity – for instance, they check if its hash is valid, and if the transactions in it are verified.

If everything is found to be ok, they add the new block to their respective copies of the blockchain and remove the transactions in it from their mempools. This ensures that the transactions are added to the blockchain only once.

Once all the nodes in the network add the new block to their copies of the blockchain, transactions within the block (including Alice sending 10 coins to Bob) are completed and become irreversible, and all respective blockchain account balances (including Alice's and Bob's) are refreshed accordingly in all the copies.

Throughout this process, Bob doesn't have to do anything to accept the 10 coins. His private key simply gives him the ability to access the 10 coins that arrive in his blockchain account once the transaction is complete.

A key salient feature of this process is the independent validation and addition of new blocks by nodes in the network (which happens in step 6). This ensures a truly distributed database, with no single node having authority over any other.

Another salient feature is the transparency of the blockchain. Although the whole process made use of cryptography in every step, the actual transaction information from Alice to Bob that is now stored on the blockchain isn't encrypted or obscured in any way. Anyone can view this transaction (as well as all other transactions) on the blockchain, by visiting the appropriate blockchain explorer websites such as btcscan.org for Bitcoin and etherscan.io for Ethereum. Private blockchains are exceptions to this, they usually don't openly publish transaction information.

This entire process is carried out by nodes autonomously, by running the software of the respective blockchain. The steps in this autonomous process keep repeating indefinitely, with new transactions constantly being created, broadcast, verified, and added to new blocks. The blockchain keeps getting longer and longer with each new block added to it permanently.

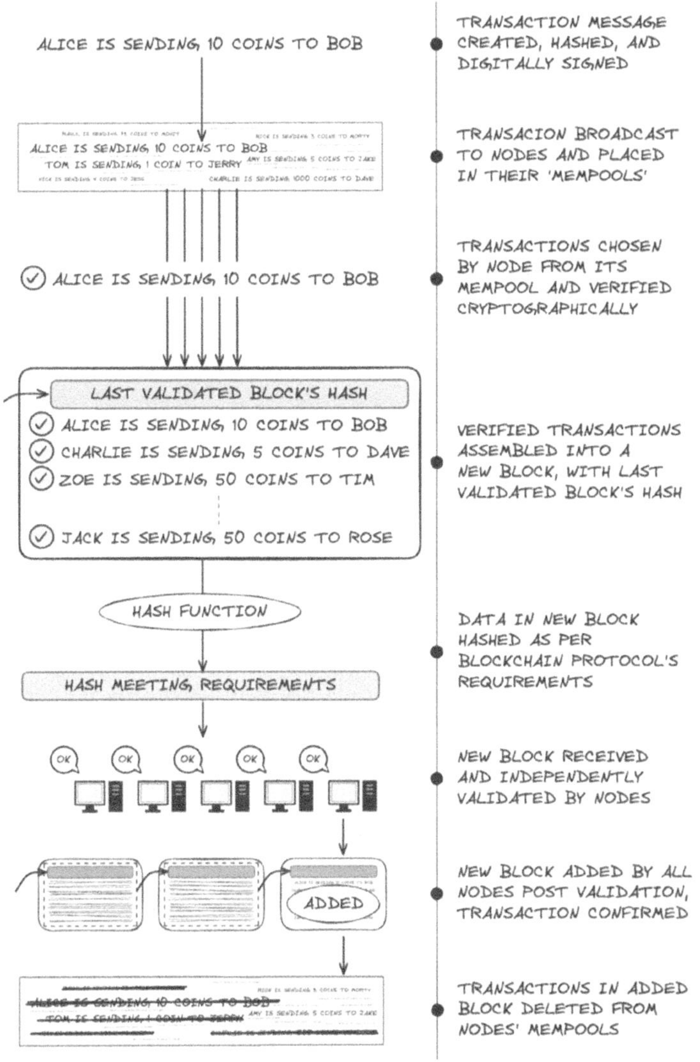
ALICE IS SENDING 10 COINS TO BOB
TRANSACTION MESSAGE CREATED, HASHED, AND DIGITALLY SIGNED
ALICE IS SENDING 10 COINS TO BOB
TOM IS SENDING 1 COIN TO JERRY
AMY IS SENDING 5 COINS TO JAKE
CHARLIE IS SENDING 1000 COINS TO DAVE
TRANSACION BROADCAST TO NODES AND PLACED IN THEIR 'MEMPOOLS'
ALICE IS SENDING 10 COINS TO BOB
TRANSACTIONS CHOSEN BY NODE FROM ITS MEMPOOL AND VERIFIED CRYPTOGRAPHICALLY
LAST VALIDATED BLOCK'S HASH
ALICE IS SENDING 10 COINS TO BOB
CHARLIE IS SENDING 5 COINS TO DAVE
ZOE IS SENDING 50 COINS TO TIM
JACK IS SENDING 50 COINS TO ROSE
VERIFIED TRANSACTIONS ASSEMBLED INTO A NEW BLOCK, WITH LAST VALIDATED BLOCK'S HASH
HASH FUNCTION
HASH MEETING REQUIREMENTS
DATA IN NEW BLOCK HASHED AS PER BLOCKCHAIN PROTOCOL'S REQUIREMENTS
OK
OK
OK
OK
OK
NEW BLOCK RECEIVED AND INDEPENDENTLY VALIDATED BY NODES
ADDED
NEW BLOCK ADDED BY ALL NODES POST VALIDATION, TRANSACTION CONFIRMED
ALICE IS SENDING 10 COINS TO BOB
TOM IS SENDING 1 COIN TO JERRY
AMY IS SENDING 5 COINS TO JAKE
TRANSACTIONS IN ADDED BLOCK DELETED FROM NODES' MEMPOOLS

I think you'll now be able to guess how this structure helps in making data on the blockchain immutable. Any attempts to modify the contents of any block would alter its hash, breaking its link to the subsequent block (which contains the correct, unaltered hash), hence breaking the chain. So, an attempt made to alter any block would have to be followed up by regeneration of the hashes of all subsequent blocks to maintain the sanctity of the blockchain. And even if a rogue node operator somehow accomplishes this, its altered copy of the blockchain will be rejected by the majority of the network's nodes holding correct copies. Remember the example from chapter 2, where any student in the class making a mistake in their notes has their copy rejected and corrected by other students with the correct notes? Just like that.

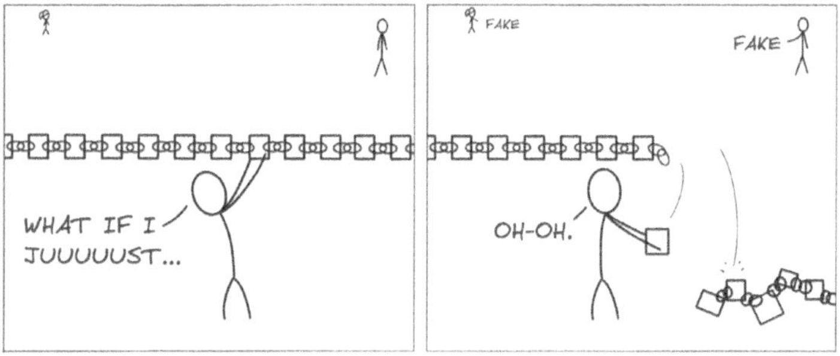

The only way for a rogue node operator to achieve this, is to take control of the majority (more than 50%) of the network and alter their blockchain copies. Then, since the majority would hold the altered copy of the blockchain, that would be considered valid. Such attacks are called "51% attacks", and these are nearly impossible to execute on large blockchains due to the massive costs involved.

That, in a nutshell, is how cryptography is used in blockchains to verify and add data to them, and to make them secure and immutable.

Please note that we used an example of a cryptocurrency transaction here, but it works similarly in all blockchain applications. The only difference is the type of information that is added – it was "Alice is sending 10 coins to Bob" in our cryptocurrency example, but could be different, e.g., "Product code 10212 received at New York hub at 13/05/2022, 12:34 am" for a supply chain management application.

5.

CONSENSUS MECHANISMS: WHO MAKES THE BLOCKS?

In the previous chapter, we briefly touched upon the step of creating a hash for a new block and adding it to the blockchain – "Step 5: … The node then finds a hash for this new block, following certain requirements …".

These requirements are defined in the blockchain's 'consensus mechanism'. **A consensus mechanism of a blockchain is a set of rules that define how data is added to it, and how its nodes reach agreement on the validity of this data.** Each node in the blockchain's network must follow these rules, to ensure the harmony of the network.

Every blockchain has its own specific twist on its consensus mechanism, so there are several different unique ones out there. Broadly though, the two most popular consensus mechanisms are 'Proof of Work' (PoW) and 'Proof of Stake' (PoS). These two (along with their variations and hybrids) govern the vast majority of the blockchains operational today.

Proof of Work (PoW)

The Proof of Work (PoW) consensus mechanism works as an open-for-all race to find a new block's hash. In this race, all participating nodes work independently to create the next block and find its hash.

Each participating node chooses multiple transactions from its respective mempool, cryptographically verifies them, and adds the hash of the last block from its copy of the blockchain to this set of verified transactions to make a new block.

Next, it finds this new block's hash as per a specific requirement which makes this process computationally difficult. For instance, in the Bitcoin protocol, the hash needs to be less than a 'difficulty target' value.

To achieve this, it uses an approach of guesswork: it includes a random number called a 'nonce' within the block's data and generates the block's hash. The nonce is iterated randomly (or, guessed repeatedly) until a hash that satisfies the requirement is generated. Recall from the previous chapter, even a minor change in the input to a hash function dramatically changes the output hash. This is what happens here, when a small part of the block's data (the nonce) is changed in every input iteration for generating the block's hash. This iterative process has often been called solving "complex math problems" or "exciting puzzles" in various media-affected descriptions. In reality, it's neither complex nor exciting, rather it's repetitive and boring.

The first node to generate a hash that meets the requirement wins the race. As soon as such a hash is generated, the winning node broadcasts the block (including the winning nonce) along with this hash to the network. All the other nodes in the network then independently validate the block by hashing it to check if it indeed yields the given hash, and checking the sanctity of the transactions included in it, e.g., if none of them are invalid or repeated. If everything is found to be ok, they add this new block to their copies of the blockchain and delete the transactions included in this block from their mempools.

Once a new block is added, the race re-starts for the next block. Each node now needs to pick up a new set of unverified transactions from its mempool, verify them, and so on.

Nodes are incentivized to participate in this race because they stand to gain two major rewards for each winning block. First, they earn a 'block reward' through a special 'coinbase' transaction that they are allowed to add to their blocks before hashing them, to pay themselves with newly created (or 'minted') cryptocurrency. And second, they collect transaction fees, or 'gas fees', from all transactions in their winning blocks. Gas fees are payments from users like Alice, who offer these fees to get their transactions added to the blockchain on priority. In fact, nodes are not obligated to add any transactions to their blocks at all, and can just create blocks with only the coinbase transaction to claim block rewards. They choose to add transactions to their blocks because they earn gas fees from doing so.

In PoW, this process of adding blocks is called 'mining', and the participating nodes are called 'miners'. This is because it is akin to spending resources (computing power) to gain assets (cryptocurrencies), much like mining in the physical world.

The more computing power a miner has, the faster it can run iterations to generate hashes, and hence the higher are the chances for it to win the race and earn rewards. But this obviously comes with higher energy consumption and hence higher cost.

The energy consumption in PoW blockchains is indeed massive, comparable to whole countries' consumptions when totalled in cases like Bitcoin with its thousands of miners. This has often caught the eye of sustainability advocates, for instance, Elon Musk stopped Tesla accepting Bitcoin payments until it becomes more sustainable, which coincidentally marked the start of the 2021 cryptocurrency market crash.

Proof of Stake (PoS)

The Proof of Stake (PoS) consensus mechanism works as a democracy, where power to create new blocks is determined by extent of investment in the network. In this mechanism, one participating node is chosen to make (or, 'propose') the next block. The probability of a node being chosen is proportional to the amount of the blockchain's native cryptocurrency it has locked up, or 'staked', in the blockchain's protocol to indicate its participation. For example, if a node owns 5% of the total cryptocurrency staked in the protocol, it has a 5% chance of being selected to propose the next block.

When a node is chosen to propose the next block, it picks up a set of transactions from its mempool, verifies them, adds the hash of the last block from its copy of the blockchain, computes this new block's hash, and broadcasts it to the network. A subset of nodes in the network (also chosen fresh for each block with probability proportional to staked cryptocurrency amounts) validate the block.

Once the new block is validated by the chosen nodes, all nodes in the network are prompted to add the new block to their copies of the blockchain and remove the included transactions from their mempools. The node which proposed the block is rewarded with gas fees from the transactions included in the block, and in some cases, newly minted cryptocurrency called a 'staking reward'. The exact reward mechanism can vary between different PoS-based blockchains.

In PoS, this process of adding blocks is called 'forging', and the participating nodes are called 'validators', which describes their roles of making and checking blocks in the blockchain.

Forging blocks in PoS is far less energy-consuming than mining blocks in PoW. In PoS, nodes don't need to use computational power to iteratively generate block hashes, unlike in PoW. The cost of participating in a PoS blockchain as a validator is not energy, rather it is acquiring and staking the native cryptocurrency of the blockchain.

PoS has its own downsides, such as potential inequality and centralization. Individuals or entities owning large amounts of staked cryptocurrency in the protocol can have disproportionate control over the network, and can influence data that goes into the blockchain, e.g. by deliberately not adding transactions from certain accounts.

To mitigate these downsides, most PoS blockchains deploy mechanisms where validators are de-incentivized for any unwanted behaviour by taking away, or 'slashing' their staked cryptocurrency. This keeps the blockchain in check.

There have been extensive debates as to which of these two mechanisms – PoW or PoS – is the better one. The winner is a question of personal preference, really. Some prefer the robust security and proven track record of PoW, while others advocate the efficiency of PoS for broader environmental concerns.

Bitcoin, the first blockchain, runs on a PoW consensus mechanism. Ethereum officially switched from PoW to PoS in 2022. Some newer blockchains like Decred, run on hybrids of PoW and PoS, to get the best of both worlds.

All consensus mechanisms ultimately take different paths to achieve the same goal, which is to ensure that consensus is achieved in the network. For a block to be completely finalized, all the nodes (miners/validators) must add the block to their blockchain copies. In cases where a few nodes add different blocks at the same position, those blocks get discarded as part of a temporary fork, which we will look at in the next chapter.

It's worthwhile to note that aside from PoW and PoS which govern the vast majority of the blockchains operational today, there are also more niche consensus mechanisms out there. For instance, Proof of Authority (PoA) grants rights to generate new blocks to nodes that are deemed trustworthy, and Proof of Capacity (PoC) grants rights to generate new blocks to nodes who use their available disk space to support the network. Covering all these in detail is a vast undertaking and will warrant a separate book, so we will skip them in this one.

Before we move on...

Here is a consolidated list of block characteristics with their basic definitions. You will often encounter these in technical conversations about blockchains.

1. **Block Height** (or simply, **Height**): The position of a block in the blockchain sequence. The genesis (first) block is at height zero, with each subsequent block increasing in height.
2. **Block Size**: The physical size of the block, typically measured in kilobytes or megabytes, determining the amount of data it can contain.
3. **Timestamp**: The time at which the block was created, maintaining the block sequence.
4. **Block Time**: The average time interval between the creation and addition of new blocks in the blockchain. It is often targeted to remain relatively constant, for instance, Bitcoin targets a block time of 10 minutes.
5. **Difficulty Target**: The maximum allowable hash value for a new block, which dictates the mining difficulty. This is adjusted frequently to maintain a consistent block time. This is only relevant in PoW blockchains, not PoS blockchains.
6. **Nonce**: A variable number iterated and added to a block to achieve its hash that meets the difficulty target requirement. This is only relevant in PoW blockchains, not PoS blockchains.
7. **Merkle Root**: A single hash representing all the transaction data in a particular block, without

including the nonce, previous block's hash, timestamp, and difficulty target. The merkle root is derived from the **Merkle Tree**, where transactions are paired, hashed, and then these hashes are paired and hashed again and so on, continuing until only a single hash remains: which is the merkle root.

8. **Block Header**: Contains metadata about the block, including the merkle root, nonce, previous block's hash, timestamp, and difficulty target.
9. **Block Hash**: The hash of everything in a block, including all the transaction data, nonce, previous block's hash, timestamp, and difficulty target. In most blockchains, the block hash is the hash of only the block header, which indirectly includes all the transaction data in the block through the merkle root. Using the merkle root (and not all the transaction data directly) makes the underlying process more efficient and secure, and allows for easier scalability of the blockchain.
10. **Block Reward**: The cryptocurrency reward claimed by a node for successfully creating a valid block. In PoS blockchains, this is often called 'staking reward'.

Please note, the above list mentions 'transaction data', but this could be any other type of data in a block, such as messages, images, product records, ID records, etc. depending on the blockchain's specific architecture and applications.

6.

FORKS IN BLOCKCHAINS

So now you know how blocks are made – participating nodes choose transactions from their mempools, verify them, and add them to blocks, which are then appended to the blockchain following rules defined in its consensus mechanism. But, you might ask, with the thousands of participating nodes operational on the network, what happens if two (or more) nodes choose different sets of transactions from their mempools and use them to make different but equally valid blocks at the same block height?

Turns out, this is indeed possible, leading to 'temporary forks'. **A temporary fork is a situation where two (or more) valid blocks are made by different nodes at the same block height, causing the blockchain to branch (or, 'fork') in different directions.** As the name suggests, this situation is only temporary and each consensus mechanism has a method to resolve it.

In PoW blockchains like Bitcoin, temporary forks happen when two miners find acceptable hashes for new blocks at the same height, and then broadcast these blocks simultaneously or within a very short timeframe. Since it might take some time for these broadcasted blocks to propagate across the network due to latency, different miners may receive, validate, and add different blocks at the same height, leading to temporary forks.

PoW resolves temporary forks by following the longest chain rule, which means that the version of the blockchain with the highest number of blocks (or more specifically, with the most cumulative computational work done on it) available with the network is chosen as the valid one.

When a miner successfully mines a new block on one of the forks and makes it longer than the others, the network must converge on this chain as the correct one, as a rule. Miners on shorter forks realize that their path is not the accepted one when they notice that incoming blocks don't include the hash of any of the blocks in their copy, prompting them to update their copy to the longer, accepted chain. Forked blocks from the shorter chain(s) are discarded, becoming 'orphan' blocks. Transactions in these orphan blocks that are not included in the longer chain return to mempools and are carried-forward for inclusion and confirmation in future blocks.

In Bitcoin's context, it is recommended to wait for the addition of 6 subsequent blocks after making a transaction to ensure its confirmation and reliability, this significantly reduces the likelihood of the transaction becoming part of an orphan block in a temporary fork.

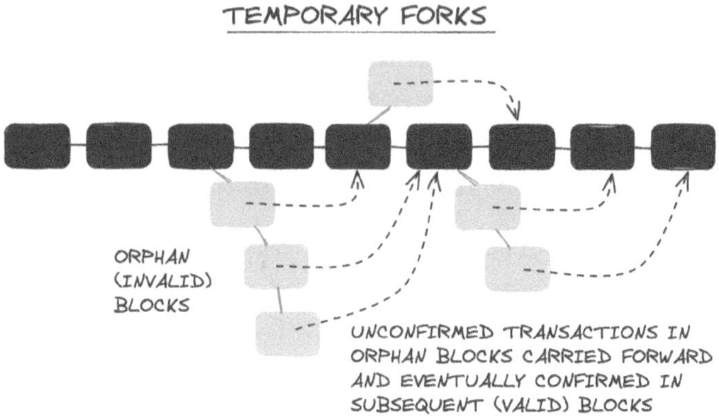

Like in PoW, temporary forks and orphan blocks also occur in PoS blockchains when two or more blocks are proposed for the same height. This can happen due to network latency, when a chosen validator is not aware that a block has already been proposed for the current height, leading them to propose another block at the same height. It can also happen if malicious or faulty validators intentionally propose multiple blocks for the same height as part of an attack or due to a bug.

The resolution of temporary forks on PoS blockchains is based on 'stake weight' – blocks on the fork made by nodes having a higher total stake take precedence, and blocks on the other forks are orphaned. Additionally, many PoS protocols incorporate 'slashing' conditions where nodes are penalized by taking away their staked cryptocurrency for behaviors that could lead to forks or for supporting multiple competing chains, further securing the network against inconsistencies.

That, in a nutshell, is how temporary forks are created and resolved. But, what if the situations leading to forks are not resolvable? For instance, what happens if the network deeply disagrees on the blockchain's established rules, and wants to go in entirely different paths? In such situations, a portion (or sometimes even the entirety) of the network might decide to follow a new direction with different rules. This leads to the creation of **'permanent forks', which represent a permanent change in the underlying rules of the blockchain protocol.** Like the name suggests, these forks cannot be reversed or resolved. Permanent forks are of two types: soft and hard.

Soft forks are backward-compatible protocol upgrades which work in a way that nodes running older protocol versions can still participate in the network without needing to update their software. This type of fork allows the blockchain to adopt new functionalities while maintaining continuity, as nodes not yet upgraded can still process new data to a degree. It's like choosing not to update your phone's OS. You can still use your phone but you'll miss out on some functionalities that the new OS offers. Technically, soft forks don't really 'fork' the blockchain, but continue it forward with new rules.

An example of a soft fork is the Taproot update in the Bitcoin blockchain in 2021, which was designed to improve efficiency and privacy of the Bitcoin protocol.

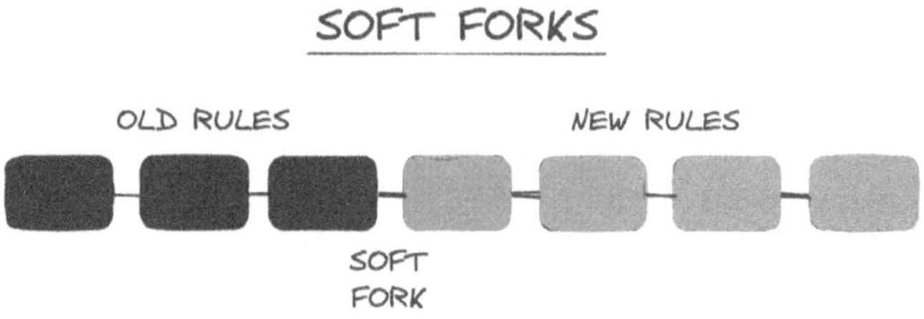

Hard forks are non-backward-compatible protocol upgrades which require all nodes to accept them to continue participating in the network. Hard forks result in a permanent split in the blockchain if all nodes don't agree to the protocol upgrades and don't update their software. This is like your phone's manufacturer requiring you to update its OS to be able to use any of the new apps on the store. You and your friends can still choose not to update your OS, but will have to develop and manage your own separate community and set of apps on the old OS, without any support from the manufacturer anymore.

An example of a hard fork is the creation of Bitcoin Cash from Bitcoin in 2017 after the SegWit update to the Bitcoin protocol. While SegWit aimed to improve transaction scalability indirectly by altering how data was stored in blocks, a substantial faction within the network advocated for a direct increase in block size. This ultimately led to a split in the community and the birth of the Bitcoin Cash blockchain. If you trace back both Bitcoin and Bitcoin Cash blockchains, you'll eventually arrive at the same block (at block height 478,558), at which the hard fork happened.

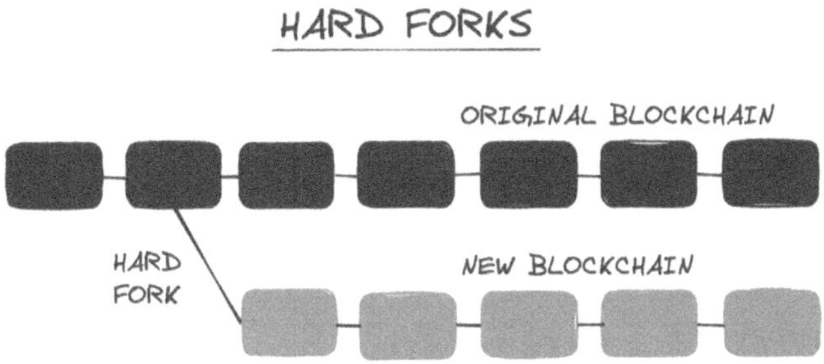

Permanent forks, both soft and hard, underscore the vital role of community in the evolution of blockchain technology. They emerge from collective discussions, debates, and decisions, highlighting the democratic ethos at the heart of blockchain development. Whether introducing new features or addressing divergent views through soft or hard forks, these moments crystallize the power of community consensus in steering the direction of the technology. They not only reflect the community's capacity to adapt and innovate but also its commitment to maintaining a decentralized and participatory approach to blockchain governance and evolution.

7.

SMART CONTRACTS: AUTONOMOUS TRUST MODELS ON BLOCKCHAINS

Smart contracts are autonomous, self-executing agreements whose terms and conditions are embedded directly into lines of code. Rather than paper trails tucked away in drawers (like in traditional, physical contracts), smart contracts live on blockchains and reap the benefits of this technology, which grants them some rather compelling features: they're transparent, irreversible, and tamper-proof.

Not all blockchains support the creation of smart contracts, especially the older ones like Bitcoin and Litecoin that have limited 'scripting' capabilities and were designed to be primarily transaction ledgers. However, almost all recent blockchains support and thrive on smart contracts, underscoring blockchain technology's increasing utility, relevance, and acceptance across an increasing number of industries today.

Smart contracts can be coded to carry out many types of agreements or transactions, involving digital or even physical assets. Let's understand this with an example: Alice wants to rent Bob's apartment for a few days.

In the traditional way, they use an intermediary platform, like Airbnb. The platform, managed by humans behind the scenes, maintains a database of apartment listings, tariffs, and availabilities. When Alice makes a query, Airbnb informs her about available apartments for the desired days. Alice selects Bob's apartment and pays Airbnb to make her booking. Airbnb, after deducting its fee, forwards the remainder to Bob. Once Bob acknowledges his payment, he arranges a means, perhaps personally or via a mailbox, to hand over the apartment keys (physical or digital) to Alice. Any discrepancies in the entire process are managed by Airbnb customer support, which typically involves Alice or Bob speaking to an Airbnb-affiliated human.

With a smart contract, this entire process is coded and happens without any intermediaries. The apartment listing data is stored on a blockchain (or on a database which the blockchain can access). Alice directly interacts with the smart contract, which presents her with a list of apartments available for her specified dates. Upon selecting Bob's apartment, she proceeds to make the payment, in cryptocurrency, to Bob's blockchain account via the smart contract. Once the payment is confirmed, the smart contract provides Alice the digital keys to Bob's apartment (or tells her where to find the physical keys). The smart contract is designed to handle any deviations from the agreed terms autonomously. For instance, if Alice fails to complete the payment, it automatically withholds the keys, ensuring compliance with the agreed conditions.

Smart contracts can be written in a variety of programming languages, such as Solidity, Python, and Vyper. Once a smart contract is written and deployed on a supporting blockchain, it is allotted an 'address', which serves the purpose of identifying it. These smart contract addresses bear resemblance to blockchain account addresses, which are usually represented as hexadecimal numbers.

'Interacting' with a smart contract simply means sending a special transaction to the contract's address. Recall the process we covered in chapter 4 – it happens exactly like that, except the transaction message contains specific instructions that trigger certain predefined actions in the smart contract. When the blockchain network processes this special transaction and adds it to a block, the smart contract's code is executed based on these instructions. This execution might involve transferring cryptocurrency, updating the contract's state, or, in the context of our apartment-renting example, triggering the release of digital keys. The entire process is secured and validated by the blockchain's network, ensuring the contract's terms are automatically fulfilled.

From a user interface (UI) point of view, users typically interact with smart contracts through decentralized applications (DApps) to which they are plugged, and using connection tools such as Metamask or WalletConnect. We'll cover DApps in detail in chapter 18.

Smart contracts are all about trust, or rather, the fact that you don't need to rely on it. The code ensures every party holds up their end of the bargain. These digital agreements aren't just confined to straightforward transactions. Their flexibility enables them to manage complex operations, from distributing royalties among musicians to facilitating intricate supply chain operations. An artist, for example, can use a smart contract to sell music directly, ensuring the revenue is fairly divided between producers, writers, and performers, all without a record label taking its traditional sizable cut.

Apart from powering these different types of utility, smart contracts are also used to create and represent new cryptocurrencies. In fact, more than 80% of the cryptocurrencies existing today are underpinned by smart contracts on existing blockchains. These are called 'tokens' and we will learn more about them in chapter 12.

Smart contracts have proved to be an extremely effective innovation which massively expanded blockchain technology's reach and relevance, but at the same time they have had their fair share of shortcomings and risks. In recent times especially, there have been instances where numerous smart contracts have been exploited, both in their concept and execution, and used for malicious intent resulting in loss or theft of cryptocurrencies.

Developers often 'renounce' smart contracts after deploying them, to add legitimacy to their projects. 'Renouncing' a smart contract is an irreversible process of giving up ownership of it, so that it cannot be altered anymore. This is done to build confidence in project investors that the developers won't alter the smart contract later for their own benefit. But this also means that coding mistakes can no longer be corrected. There have been instances of unintentional bugs being exploited in renounced smart contracts, leading to huge amounts of cryptocurrencies being stolen from legitimate projects.

Malicious smart contracts have also been often designed by scammers to look like legitimate services, but intended to drain cryptocurrencies from blockchain accounts that interact with them.

Last but not the least, the legal/regulatory standing of smart contracts remains a grey area in many parts of the world, since they are generally not registered or insured by any authority.

Nonetheless, it won't be a stretch to say that smart contracts have the centerstage in the future of blockchain technology. They are the building blocks of Web3 (the new era of the internet), serving not only as trust automation tools but also as the backbone for decentralized utility, ownership, and interaction. They are central to evolving a more secure, transparent, and user-centric digital ecosystem, marking a significant shift towards a decentralized online world.

8.

BLOCKCHAIN INDUSTRY USE CASES

Blockchain technology has rapidly evolved over the last decade and a half. Its features, especially decentralization, immutability and transparency, make it an ideal solution for various industry challenges. Of course, cryptocurrencies are its first and most extensive application (so far), but before we dive into those in the next unit, let's explore some promising use cases of blockchain technology across different sectors.

Firstly, speaking of cryptocurrencies, the **financial services** industry has been harnessing blockchain technology for various other purposes beyond cryptocurrencies. International transactions, known for their low speeds and high costs, can be significantly improved with blockchains. They offer faster, more secure, and cheaper cross-border payments by bypassing traditional banking networks. Blockchain's smart contracts – which are self-executing contracts with the terms directly written into code – are also revolutionizing contractual transactions, reducing the need for intermediaries and lowering the risk of fraud.

In **supply chain management**, blockchains offer unprecedented visibility and traceability. Products can be tracked from origin to consumer, providing a transparent and tamper-proof record. This capability is especially valuable in industries like pharmaceuticals and food, where provenance and safety are paramount. For example, a blockchain can track the journey of perishable food products all the way from production to retail, verifying authenticity, ensuring appropriate storage conditions, and providing traceable timelines. This kind of robust oversight significantly reduces the risk of expired food making its way to consumers, enhancing food safety and quality assurance.

Real estate is benefiting from blockchain technology through 'asset tokenization', which involves dividing property into tradable shares or non-fungible tokens (NFTs). This approach lowers barriers to real estate investment, allowing for fractional ownership and making it more accessible. Moreover, blockchains can streamline property transactions, reducing the need for paper-based processes and making transactions more efficient and transparent.

Healthcare is another sector where blockchain technology is making significant inroads. Patient data management is a critical area, often plagued by issues of accessibility, security, and interoperability. Blockchains can securely store patient records, granting access only to authorized individuals and ensuring data integrity. In research and drug development, blockchains can manage and securely share vast amounts of certified-authentic clinical trial data, facilitating collaboration while maintaining confidentiality.

In the **energy** sector, blockchain technology is facilitating the shift towards decentralized energy systems. It enables peer-to-peer energy trading, allowing consumers with renewable energy sources like solar panels and windmills to sell excess energy directly to neighbours without going through the traditional grid. This not only empowers consumers but also promotes the use of renewable energy.

The **education** sector is utilizing blockchains to manage and verify academic credentials. By storing degrees and certificates on a blockchain, educational institutions make it easier for employers to verify qualifications, reducing fraud and simplifying recruitment processes.

Blockchain's potential is not limited to these industries. It's being explored in fields as diverse as voting systems, where it can offer secure and transparent election processes, in the art world, where it helps in authenticating and tracing the ownership of artworks, and in insurance, by automating claims processing with smart contracts.

As industries continue to explore and adopt blockchain technology, its potential to transform traditional business models and operational processes becomes increasingly evident. The technology is not just a tool for efficiency, it is also a catalyst for innovation, opening new avenues for business and societal advancements. As we move forward, blockchain technology's role in various sectors is poised to grow, continually reshaping the way we interact with the world around us.

CRYPTOCURRENCIES

9.

LET'S TALK CRYPTOCURRENCIES

In the previous unit about blockchain fundamentals, cryptocurrencies came up a few times. We covered how blockchain technology underpins cryptocurrencies and saw how data is added to blockchains through an example of a cryptocurrency transaction. Our focus there was on understanding the workings of blockchain technology. We haven't yet properly talked about what cryptocurrencies are, where they came from, and how they work.

In a nutshell, **cryptocurrencies are digital assets that use blockchains as their transaction ledgers.** To fully understand how cryptocurrencies came into being, it is essential to know the basics of money and how it evolved, so let's take a rapid-fire history lesson of that.

The earliest transactions in which humankind engaged were through the barter system, which involved exchanging things that had value, e.g., sheep for vases. The barter system wasn't a good way to operate, as it needed very specific matches of supply and demand at the commodity level for each transaction to happen seamlessly. Just picture Carol, with her surplus of sheep, trying to barter with Dave, who didn't need or want any sheep. Such conundrums with the barter system ushered in the concept of 'money'.

Money is basically a store of value and a universal medium of exchange. Slowly, the barter system gave way to the age of money. Things were assigned quantitative values based on their demand and supply, and appropriate amounts of money were exchanged for them.

Initially, objects that were relatively unique or scarce were used as money, e.g., seashells. We slowly graduated to minting metallic coins, and then to printing paper money. With the advent of the digital era, we now have digital money, that's what you use when you tap your credit card at a point of sale (POS) or send a payment using PayTM or Venmo.

All these forms of money – coins, paper and digital – are issued by an authority, usually a government or a central bank affiliated to one. This money has value because the government assigns value to it. Every country has its own version of government-backed money, called its 'currency'. **Official currencies backed by governments are referred to as 'fiat' currencies.**

In an ideal world, money issued by governments and facilitated by intermediaries such as banks, works fine. In the real world though, inefficiencies in these entities' workings often cause inconvenience to people. In worst case scenarios, mismanagement of processes and/or assets by these entities leads to large scale financial crises where people can lose money through no fault of their own, like what happened back in 2008. These concerns with traditional money prompted the birth of cryptocurrencies.

Cryptocurrencies represent an evolution of digital money, harnessing decentralization using blockchain technology. Like the forms of money that we talked about so far, cryptocurrencies were originally created to serve as stores of value and mediums of exchange. However, unlike traditional money, they are not issued or assigned value by any authority, rather they are run solely using computer code, and their value is derived from collective belief and trust. This value derivation happens mathematically and/or algorithmically, don't visualize a townhall of trusted people regularly getting together to assign value to cryptocurrencies.

Circling back to what we started this book with – "The words 'blockchain' and 'cryptocurrency' are often subconsciously entangled" – well, this is for a reason. The two emerged simultaneously in 2008 with Bitcoin, the first cryptocurrency, which was also the first pragmatic implementation of blockchain technology. Bitcoin was a response to the 2008 financial crisis, banking collapses, and the perceived mishandling of financial trust. Through the merits of blockchain, it was designed to be decentralized, with transactions verified by nodes using cryptography, eliminating the need for third parties like banks.

With Bitcoin leading from the front, the crypto-world soon expanded. In 2011, Litecoin was introduced as the "silver to Bitcoin's gold", using a different hashing algorithm and offering faster transaction times. Then in 2012 came Ripple with its cryptocurrency XRP, focused on enabling secure and instant global transactions through its digital payment protocol. Dogecoin was launched in 2013 as a light-hearted take on Bitcoin. Initially introduced as a joke based on the 'Doge' meme, it gained a lot of traction and has seen significant usage.

Then in 2015, Ethereum entered the scene, bringing along not just a cryptocurrency called Ether, but also a platform for creating smart contracts. Please note the important distinction between "Ethereum" which is a blockchain, and "Ether", which is its native cryptocurrency. Informally, the cryptocurrency Ether is often called "Ethereum" or "Ethereum coin", but we're not doing so in this book.

Through smart contracts, Ethereum introduced an easy way for setting up and launching new cryptocurrencies on the blockchain, which was the real point of explosion in the number of existing cryptocurrencies. The list grew quickly, and with more blockchains supporting smart contracts such as Cardano, Binance, and Solana following hot on Ethereum's heels, their applications broadened.

Today, there are thousands of cryptocurrencies in operation on hundreds of blockchains. And while they were initially intended to be stores of value and mediums of exchange, they have become more popular as an asset class (or an investment vehicle) while simultaneously powering different kinds of utility enabling a plethora of blockchain applications in a variety of industries.

The meteoric rise of cryptocurrencies has seen a boat-load of controversies and challenges. While many have hailed them as an inflation-hedging asset or even the future of money, critics have pointed out the volatile nature of crypto prices, the significant potential for their misuse, and environmental concerns, especially with energy-intensive consensus mechanisms in some blockchains. Amidst all these debates though, one fact remains clear: cryptocurrencies have firmly established themselves in the financial landscape. The thousands of cryptocurrencies available today, from the titans like Bitcoin and Ether to newer niche tokens, signify a diverse and vibrant ecosystem.

The decade and a half long journey from Bitcoin to thousands represents the start of the next exciting chapter in humankind's saga of trade and value storage. The world of cryptocurrencies is still at a nascent stage, and the future promises even more evolution, innovation, and one day inevitably, some more rapid-fire history

10.

THE BITCOIN STORY

Bitcoin was the first cryptocurrency, and the story of its inception reads like the plot of a thriller. Mysterious protagonists (who, to this day, remain unknown), ground-breaking innovation, and financial revolutions all form the backdrop of this narrative.

The year was 2008. The world was reeling from a massive financial crisis, banks were collapsing, trust in traditional financial systems was at an all-time low, and amidst this chaos, an anonymous figure (or a group, we may never know for sure) going by the pseudonym 'Satoshi Nakamoto' published a whitepaper titled "Bitcoin: A Peer-to-Peer Electronic Cash System".

In this whitepaper, Satoshi conceptualized a decentralized digital currency system underpinned by cryptography, where transactions happen without intermediaries. This system formed the basis of blockchain technology, although the whitepaper itself did not mention the word 'blockchain'. It also introduced 'Bitcoin' as the currency of this system. Unlike traditional currencies backed by governments, Bitcoin lives on the blockchain and is backed by algorithms defined in this whitepaper.

After publishing the whitepaper, Satoshi actively engaged with the online cryptography community through forums like the Cryptography Mailing List and BitcoinTalk, all the while remaining anonymous himself. During this time, he refined Bitcoin's concepts and recruited volunteer developers who worked on translating the whitepaper's theories into functional code. This collaborative development and testing proved to be very effective for ensuring the code's functionality and the blockchain's effective decentralized operation.

Bitcoin's anatomy was detailed during this development phase. Each Bitcoin is divisible into 100 million smaller units called 'Satoshis', representing its smallest denomination. Which means it's possible to deal in fractions of Bitcoins up to the 8th decimal place but not beyond that, because it's not possible to break a Satoshi into any further fractions.

The Bitcoin blockchain pioneered the Proof of Work (PoW) consensus mechanism, in which node operators who use their computational resources to verify transactions and successfully add them to blocks get Bitcoins as 'block rewards', we covered this concept in chapter 5. This process of 'mining' blocks provided both a way to create (or 'mint') new Bitcoins and an incentive for people to setup miner nodes and contribute computing power to the network.

Bitcoin's protocol was designed so that block rewards are the only way for new Bitcoins to be minted and introduced into the market. Further, a novel concept which is integral to this protocol is **'Bitcoin halving', a**

process which cuts block rewards by half after every 210,000 blocks are mined. Each time-period of 210,000 blocks being mined is called a 'halving cycle'.

Bitcoin halving was designed to regulate the minting and introduction of new Bitcoins into the market, and to enhance its scarcity at the same time. The initial block rewards from mining were programmed to start at 50 Bitcoins per block. These will continue to be progressively cut by half after every halving cycle, till they reduce to a Satoshi (10^{-8} Bitcoin) per block, which is not divisible any further. This will happen in the 33rd halving cycle, and after this cycle the block rewards will stop altogether.

Lastly, the mining difficulty of blocks on the Bitcoin blockchain is tweaked after every 2016 blocks by adjusting the target maximum threshold for its block hashes. This is done to ensure that the rate of mining is maintained at roughly a block every 10 minutes.

Putting all these protocol features together, it means that each Bitcoin halving event happens roughly every 4 years, and that there is a hard cap of ~21 million (more precisely, 20,999,999.9769) on the total number of Bitcoins that can ever exist. If the protocol is never modified, the last sliver of the last Bitcoin will be minted in the year 2140, more than a century from now. Beyond that point, there will be no block rewards, and miners will only be incentivized by transaction (gas) fees. This long-term scarcity of Bitcoin that is enforced by its elegant protocol is core to its economic appeal of being inflation resistant.

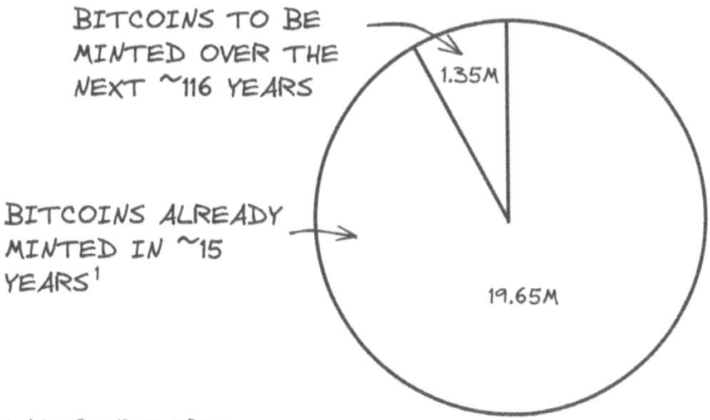

With all these protocol features designed and cemented into functional code by Satoshi's league of voluntary developers, 3rd January 2009 is when it all went live with the creation of the first Bitcoin block, aptly named the 'Genesis Block'. Satoshi left a message in this block, quoting The Times' headline from the same day – "The Times 03/Jan/2009 Chancellor on brink of second bailout for banks". It was both a timestamp and a stark reminder of the financial turmoil from which Bitcoin emerged.

In 2011, Satoshi Nakamoto effectively disappeared. The last known communication attributed to Satoshi was an email to one of the volunteer developers in April 2011, in which he mentioned moving on to other things and left the ongoing development of Bitcoin in the hands of the community. After this point, no verified communication from Satoshi has been reported, and his identity remains one of the most intriguing mysteries of the internet.

Despite its revolutionary design, Bitcoin's early days were very modest. For a while, it remained known only as an experiment in tech and cryptography circles online. Earning Bitcoin as block rewards from mining was easy at the outset and could be done on a personal computer, since there were only a few miners in the network, so its target difficulty for hashing blocks and hence the computational power requirement was very low. Buying Bitcoin directly in exchange for fiat currency, on the other hand, was very difficult, with only a few websites like BitcoinMarket.com selling it online.

The first notable commercial transaction with Bitcoin was a purchase of two pizzas for 10,000 Bitcoins by a Florida-based programmer names Laszlo Hanyecz, on 22nd May, 2010. 22nd May is now celebrated as 'Bitcoin Pizza Day' every year to commemorate this transaction.

In 2011, Bitcoin found its first extensive use case in Silk Road, an infamous online black market, as a mode of anonymous payments. While Silk Road was swiftly dismantled by authorities, it inadvertently did contribute to Bitcoin's early notoriety and its recognition as a digital asset with real-world value, and there was no looking back after that.

In just a few years, Bitcoin became mainstream enough for there to be a vast network of 'exchanges' facilitating people to buy it on the internet. Additionally, 'Bitcoin ATMs' emerged globally, allowing transactions in Bitcoin for fiat currencies.

Fast forward to today, Bitcoin has transcended its modest origins to become an almost household name globally. It's very easy to buy Bitcoin on the internet, with scores of centralized exchanges (CEXs) trading it for fiat currencies. But it has now become extremely difficult to earn it as block rewards, because thousands of nodes have joined the race as miners, so its target difficulty for hashing blocks and hence the computational power requirement is very high. In fact, it's so high that there are companies making specialized hardware for the explicit purpose of mining Bitcoin blocks, and the annual energy consumption of the Bitcoin blockchain exceeds that of entire countries, which has sparked sustainability debates.

Bitcoin has now become so widespread as to even gain official recognition from sovereign state governments, central banks, and financial regulators. In 2021 El Salvador became the first country to officially recognize Bitcoin as an alternate legal tender, and in 2022 The Central African Republic followed in its footsteps. At the time of writing (March 2024), Bitcoin ETFs (Exchange-Traded Funds) are available in Canada, Brazil, and the United States, further cementing Bitcoin's place as a widely recognized digital asset. Bitcoin ETFs have marked a significant shift in the investment landscape, enabling mainstream investors to gain exposure to Bitcoin in a regulated and potentially less risky way, without the complexities of directly buying and managing it.

Bitcoin hasn't just been about introducing a new currency or an asset. It has challenged our understanding of trust, centralization, and monetary systems. It has sparked a new wave of decentralized technologies and innovations. And while the true identity of Satoshi Nakamoto remains a mystery to this day, his (or their?) creation has indubitably marked the beginning of a new financial epoch.

11.

THE VAST CRYPTOCURRENCY-SPECTRUM BEYOND BITCOIN

Bitcoin's creation kick-started the cryptocurrency revolution and paved the way for the birth of a diverse range of cryptocurrencies, each with distinct technical specifications, use cases, and philosophies. Today, there are thousands of cryptocurrencies in operation on hundreds of blockchains.

We briefly mentioned a few cryptocurrencies and their use cases so far, now let's assign a method to the madness to better understand and navigate their vast ocean. One of the most obvious ways to classify cryptocurrencies is based on their objectives and use cases. From this perspective, broadly there are 5 categories of cryptocurrencies existing today.

1. **Currencies/stores-of-value:** As the name suggests, these cryptocurrencies are designed to serve as mediums exchange and stores of value. They often aim to improve upon the perceived limitations of Bitcoin. Litecoin and Dash are examples of this type of cryptocurrencies, other than Bitcoin of course.

2. **Platform coins:** These cryptocurrencies provide a foundation for building smart contracts and creating other new cryptocurrencies on the blockchains on which they operate. They offer a broader range of functionalities beyond simple transactions or value storage. Ether, Cardano, and Binance Coin and examples of platform coins.
3. **Utility tokens:** These cryptocurrencies are designed to offer specific utilities within blockchain-based projects – whether it's to access a service, drive governance, facilitate specific types of transactions, enable interoperability between blockchains, or serve other intrinsic functions. Chainlink, Maker, and Cake are examples of utility tokens.
4. **Non-fungible tokens (NFTs):** These make up a special type of cryptocurrencies that are designed to represent ownership rights to specific physical or digital/intangible assets. Their 'non-fungible' nature means each token is distinct and cannot be exchanged on a one-to-one basis for another, even within the same NFT collection. CryptoPunks and Bored Ape Yacht Club (BAYC) are examples of popular NFTs.
5. **Stablecoins:** These cryptocurrencies are designed to maintain a stable value by pegging them to another asset, usually a fiat currency like the US dollar. The idea is to combine the

benefits of digital currencies with the stability of traditional assets. Tether, TrueUSD, and USDCoin are examples of stablecoins.

The extensive use cases offered by cryptocurrencies across these five categories have been instrumental in driving the evolution of this landscape. The diverse range of cryptocurrencies has fostered continuous innovation by introducing new technologies and functionalities that Bitcoin, in its original design, did not possess. It has also promoted healthy competition in the overall landscape, pushing projects to continuously improve and adapt. Moreover, this variety offers choices to users and developers, since different cryptocurrencies cater to different user priorities – be it speed, privacy, functionality, or some other specific thing.

However, in this rapid surge, there have also been many cryptocurrencies with little to no practical utility. For example, some are 'memecoins', made just for fun based on internet jokes, without any practical purpose. Unfortunately, there have also been numerous scams posing as legitimate projects. These cryptocurrencies without use cases have become so common that they could be considered a category by themselves – the 6th one – in our classification. This situation has sparked skepticism, with critics doubting the long-term viability of cryptocurrencies. Additionally, it has brought regulatory challenges as authorities struggle to keep up with the hundreds of new cryptocurrencies that pop up every month.

The rapid rise in the number of cryptocurrencies represents the democratization of this landscape. They showcase the versatility of blockchain technology, proving that it can be tailored to fit various needs and purposes beyond the original vision of Bitcoin. While the future might see consolidation with only the truly valuable and useful cryptocurrencies surviving, their vibrant spectrum continues to be a testament to the innovative spirit of the crypto community.

12.

COINS VS TOKENS

In our classification of cryptocurrencies by use case in the previous chapter, we came across the terms 'coins' and 'tokens'. Although these two words are often used interchangeably in informal crypto-speak, they are technically different concepts.

A coin is a cryptocurrency that independently operates on its own blockchain and is often referred to as the blockchain's 'native' coin. Bitcoin, Litecoin, Ether, Solana, and Cardano all fall under this category.

The creation of a new coin requires the development of a new blockchain. The newly created coin then functions as the native coin of the new blockchain. However, the vice versa is not always true, every new blockchain doesn't necessarily require its own native coin. Sometimes, a blockchain can utilize the native coin of another associated blockchain. Furthermore, depending on their applications, several blockchains do not need native coins or indeed any cryptocurrencies on them at all.

Tokens, unlike coins, don't have their own blockchains and cannot be operated independently.

They are built on existing blockchains, which basically means that their transactions and balances are recoded on ledgers on existing blockchains. Tokens are created to drive specific utility for blockchain-based projects, for example, access to a specific amount of cloud storage can require holding a certain number of tokens.

New tokens are created through the deployment of smart contracts on blockchains that support such functionality, for instance, Ethereum and BNB Chain. Several blockchains do not support smart contracts so they can't have tokens on them, for instance Bitcoin and Litecoin blockchains. Although, 'layer-2 solutions' make it possible to indirectly create tokens associated with such blockchains, for instance the Omni layer on the Bitcoin blockchain. We'll talk about layer-2 solutions in chapter 23.

A token's smart contract specifies and enforces the rules which govern it, such as its total supply and its buying/selling mechanics. Once deployed, a token's smart contract (like any other smart contract) has a unique address on the blockchain. This address, which is typically represented as a hexadecimal number, is called the token's 'contract address', or simply its 'contract'. In essence, the contract address serves as the official location of the token on the blockchain. When blockchain accounts interact with the token, such as when buying, selling, transferring, 'minting' (creating), or 'burning' (destroying) the token, they essentially interact with the smart contract by sending transaction messages referencing this address.

Today, blockchains have become so user-friendly that anyone, irrespective of whether they know coding or not, can create their own cryptocurrency token on any supporting blockchain of their choice. Just Google "How to create your own cryptocurrency" and you'll see what I mean.

Although this is a good thing for the most part, it has inadvertently opened doors for tokens without any practical utility. Some of these are even created by malicious actors to exploit the system for personal gain. Prominent scams include 'rugpulls', where scammers allure individuals to buy their legitimate-looking tokens with promises of utility but elope with the investment, and 'honeypots', where tokens are available for purchase but cannot be sold by anyone except for their creators. As the cryptocurrency world has expanded, the prevalence of these types of tokens has increased significantly. This underpins the growing need for regulation, without which such tokens will continue to thrive, ultimately eroding trust in the broader ecosystem.

Now, before we wrap up here, let's put the distinction between coins and tokens together with the use-case based classification from the previous chapter, to create a comprehensive map.

- Currencies/stores of value are coins. Although some tokens do serve a similar purpose, their utility is confined to the specific projects for which they are created and doesn't extend across the entire blockchain network, unlike coins in this category.
- Platform coins are, by definition, coins.
- Utility tokens and NFTs are tokens (and so are the ones created without any utility or for malicious purposes).
- Stablecoins are also tokens, although they have the word 'coin' in their name.

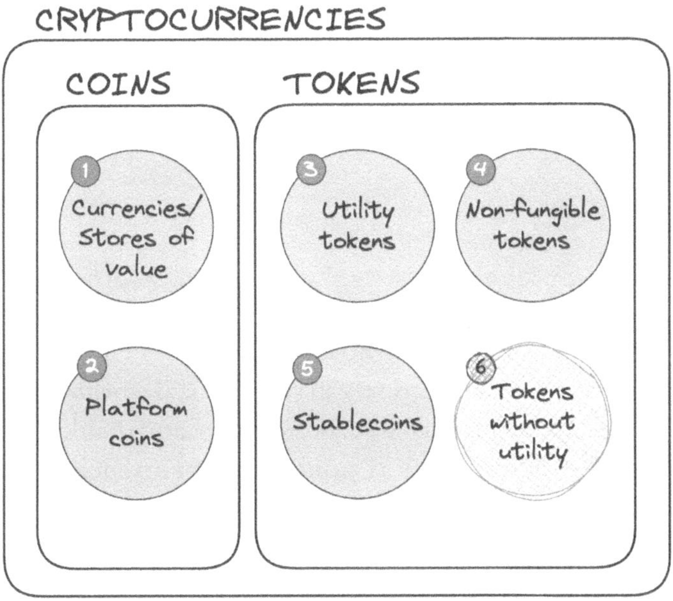

13.

WHAT IT MEANS TO 'HOLD' CRYPTOCURRENCIES

The term 'holding' in the context of financial assets means 'owning'. But what does it mean to own cryptocurrencies? For instance, what does it mean to own 1 Bitcoin? Where is this Bitcoin, exactly? On your computer? Can you store it under your mattress, like your dollar bills?

Well, first and foremost, cryptocurrencies do not and cannot exist concretely in the physical world, unlike fiat money which is issued as coins and banknotes, or unlike assets such as gold. Cryptocurrencies only exist on blockchains as account balances on ledgers. When transactions happen, these blockchain account balances change. That's the crux of it.

Holding or owning cryptocurrencies means having control over the corresponding coins or tokens in the blockchain ledger. There are two broad ways you can do that – in your own blockchain account ('non-custodially'), or in someone else's blockchain account ('custodially').

The non-custodial way

In a nutshell, **holding cryptocurrencies in the 'non-custodial' way means exclusively owning a blockchain account with the corresponding coins or tokens in it.**

We've mentioned 'blockchain accounts' several times in the book so far. Let's take a closer look at these, and what it means to 'exclusively own' one. For this, first go back and quickly refresh your memory of chapter 4 on cryptography if you need to. All set? Ok, here we go.

Simply put, **'blockchain accounts' are nothing more than ledger entries tracking cryptocurrency balances on blockchains.** As we saw in chapter 4, blockchain accounts are secured by public-key cryptography, and each one has a pair of private and public keys associated with it.

Here is a simplified overview of how blockchain accounts are set up and these keys are generated on many popular blockchains –

1. When a user requests a new blockchain account, it triggers the generation of a random private key. This is usually a 256-bit number.

The chance of generating a private key that is already in use is extremely low since there are 2^{256} possible private keys, this number is unimaginably large.

2. The public key is derived from this private key using an irreversible cryptographic function, such as elliptic curve multiplication. This is similar to hashing from the perspective of being irreversible, but is technically done using different algorithms. Being irreversible means that it's impossible to directly derive a private key from its paired public key, the only way to do so is guesswork.

3. The public key is hashed, and typically, a portion of the hash is used to create the 'address' of the blockchain account. For instance, the Ethereum blockchain creates addresses from the last 160 bits of the public key's hash. This truncation helps in maintaining shorter, more manageable addresses while still ensuring a high degree of uniqueness and security. The address is usually represented in a compact, hexadecimal format for ease of communication.

A blockchain account's address is the only attribute that uniquely identifies it in the blockchain ledger, which is like a table listing addresses alongside their respective cryptocurrency balances. When a new account is created, its address gets added to this table with zero initial balance against it.

ADDRESS	BALANCE
827A9DE1...C4	0.11224746
E3889A9...ACC	1.23324743
73772AF...8FA	20.61515371
628A931C...2A1	9.62837628
A7ABE1F5...A25	3.83728182
44CAF718...876	0.00059386
7AAD72CD...1FF	0.00000000
⋮	⋮

← NEWLY CREATED BLOCKCHAIN ACCOUNT WITH ZERO BALANCE

4. The private key is often mnemonically converted into a unique 12 or 24 word 'seed phrase' for better readability and ease of use. This seed phrase uniquely represents the private key and must be kept secure and secret by the account owner.

From a user's point of view, an address is the only thing required to identify a blockchain account, and a seed phrase is the only thing needed to have full access to it. This setup, in some ways, is similar to traditional banking. A blockchain account's address is like a bank account number, anyone can send money to it just by referencing it. And a seed phrase is like a password, you can access the contents of your account only if you know its password.

As long as you keep your seed phrase safe and secure, you are the 'exclusive owner' of your blockchain account, and no one other than you has access to its contents. This is called the 'non-custodial' way of holding cryptocurrencies because you aren't giving custody of your cryptocurrencies to anyone other than yourself. If you lose your seed phrase, you lose your blockchain account, period. Furthermore, if anyone else gets to know your seed phrase, they can access your blockchain account and transfer/spend your cryptocurrency holdings. Unlike traditional banking, there's no customer support to help you retrieve your cryptocurrencies if these situations arise.

Unlike seed phrases, addresses (which are derived from public keys) don't need to be kept secret. Addresses are public identifiers of blockchain accounts and are required to be to be referenced while making non-custodial cryptocurrency transactions. Going back to the example from chapter 4, when Alice sends

10 coins to Bob, she needs to reference both their addresses in the transaction message she creates.

Blockchains (except private ones) usually openly publish a list of addresses of all accounts ever created on them along with their real-time cryptocurrency balances and transactions. For instance, btcscan.org does that for the Bitcoin blockchain.

Ownership a blockchain account is 'pseudo-anonymous' or 'pseudonymous', because while anyone can view the real-time balances and transactions of any address, the identity of an address's owner remains undisclosed unless revealed by the owner or someone who knowingly transacts with the owner.

Users who opt for non-custodial holdings often use cryptocurrency 'wallets'. **Wallets are tools that can create blockchain accounts and execute transactions from them.** Wallets are of two types: hardware and software.

Hardware wallets resemble USB devices, and offer robust 'cold storage' solutions for cryptocurrencies by keeping private keys completely offline. Software wallets, or 'hot wallets', are applications on computers or smartphones. They are frequently connected to the internet, making them more convenient to use but also more exposed than hardware wallets.

Apart from helping easily access and transact their non-custodial cryptocurrency holdings, wallets also provide users the ability to connect their blockchain accounts with smart contracts and interact with them, using connection tools such as Metamask and WalletConnect. Users generally prefer connecting only hot wallets to smart contracts for safety reasons, transferring minimal cryptocurrency amounts from their more secure cold storage wallets to these hot wallets as necessary.

The custodial way

The second broad way to hold cryptocurrencies is the **'custodial' way, where users entrust (or give custody of) their cryptocurrencies to a third-party service,** like a centralized exchange (CEX).

CEXs are essentially cryptocurrency banks, owned and controlled by private entities. When you hold a cryptocurrency on a CEX, it is simply allocated to your CEX account (which is not a blockchain account). The CEX itself needs to hold appropriate balances in their own blockchain accounts (or legally own assets to be able to acquire the appropriate balances on short notice), to be able to match all their users' holdings on CEX accounts, this is often required by regulation.

With custodial holdings, you're relieved of the responsibility of managing your seed phrases securely. You only need to manage your CEX account password, and if you lose that, the CEX's customer support can help you recover it, much like a traditional bank operates. However, the downside of custodial holdings is that you don't fully control your cryptocurrencies, the CEX does. So, if the CEX faces hacks or bankruptcy, you risk losing your assets as they were never truly in your possession. This is like having money in a traditional bank account and losing it when the bank goes under.

There is a phrase that is thrown around quite often in crypto-speak, "Not your keys, not your crypto".

It's possible and usually quite easy to convert cryptocurrency holdings from custodial to non-custodial and vice versa. Upon creating accounts on a CEX, users are assigned unique 'deposit addresses' for each supported blockchain. The blockchain accounts corresponding to these deposit addresses are owned by the CEX, not by the user. Users can transfer their non-custodial cryptocurrency holdings to these deposit accounts, thereby making them custodial with the CEX. Conversely, to convert custodial cryptocurrency holdings to non-custodial, users can request the CEX to transfer their assets to a blockchain account they own exclusively, by providing its address.

Converting fiat currencies to cryptocurrencies and vice versa is usually done on CEXs. Users buy cryptocurrencies with fiat on CEXs, and then transfer them to their own blockchain accounts if they wish to hold non-custodially. They can also transfer cryptocurrency from their blockchain accounts to the CEX and sell it for fiat there. These days, some wallet applications and DApps also come with direct buying and selling options for popular cryptocurrencies. These mechanisms work without the need to explicitly interact with a CEX as an intermediary.

In conclusion, although you can't store your Bitcoin under your mattress, you can write down your seed phrase on a piece of paper and store it there. Many would say this is better than holding it on a CEX.

14.

HOW CRYPTOCURRENCIES ARE PRICED

Cryptocurrencies are decentralized, which means there are no authorities issuing them or backing their value. They are worth what people collectively perceive them to be, and this is quantitatively reflected in their prices through autonomous mechanisms.

The price of a cryptocurrency simply means the value of a single unit of it expressed in a fiat currency, like the US dollar (USD).

The mechanisms for determining cryptocurrency prices are fundamentally based on the economic principles of demand and supply. The demand for cryptocurrencies is driven by their perception (or what people believe they are worth). Their supply is determined by their decentralized protocols, for instance there won't ever be more than 21 million Bitcoins.

The primary mechanisms determining prices of coins (which run independently on their own blockchains) technically differ from those of tokens (which are built on existing blockchains).

Pricing mechanisms for coins

For coins (such as Bitcoin and Ether), prices are determined using 'order books' on centralized exchanges (CEXs). Yes, the same CEXs we talked about in the previous chapter's section on custodial holdings.

The order book mechanism is a foundational feature of most exchanges (cryptocurrency or stock). On a CEX, the order book is a real-time list of buy and sell orders for a particular cryptocurrency. Traders submit buy and sell orders (known as 'bids' and 'asks' respectively) on the CEX, specifying a quantity they want to trade and the price they're willing to accept. The CEX's role is to match up these bids and asks. A trade occurs when the highest bid overlaps with the lowest ask. If there is no overlap, sellers tend to lower the asks and buyers tend to increase the bids until there is an overlap, so that a trade can occur. The price at which the last trade occurred becomes the latest traded price for the cryptocurrency on that CEX.

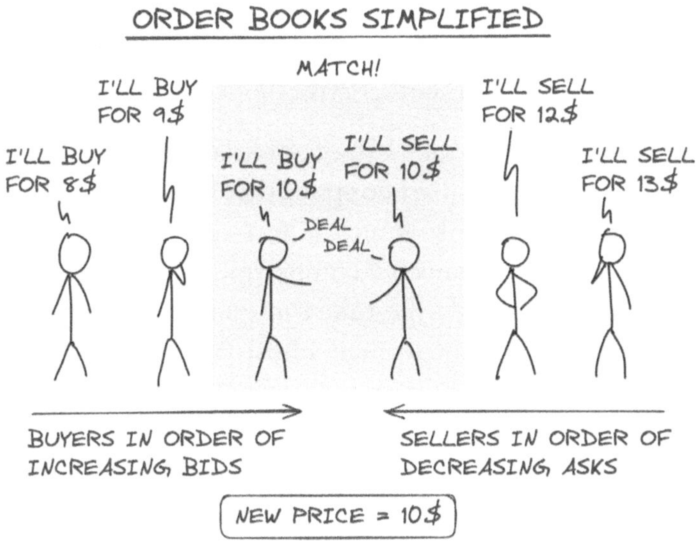

Buying and selling on order books is a primary trading mechanism used by all CEXs. In addition, CEXs also commonly make other trading mechanisms available on their platforms. For instance, many CEXs have speculative trading tools such as futures and options, which can indirectly affect the price moments by swaying market sentiments. Several CEXs also offer moderated peer to peer (P2P) trading where individual buyers and sellers set the prices for specific transactions outside order books. However, despite all these additional mechanisms, the market-level price determination on CEXs only happens on order books.

Pricing mechanisms for tokens

For tokens, their price is determined using liquidity pools (LPs) and automated market makers (AMMs) on

decentralized exchanges (DEXs), through mechanisms that are underpinned by math and reliant on stablecoins or native coins of the respective blockchains.

A 'Liquidity Pool' (LP) of a token is a collection of funds locked in a smart contract that facilitates trading of the token. Think of an LP as a special blockchain account with 2 connected compartments or sides. One of these sides holds the token in question. The other side holds a cryptocurrency whose price is externally determined by a separate mechanism, for instance by a CEX order book. This is called the token's 'paired cryptocurrency' on the LP, and it's usually a stablecoin or the native coin of the blockchain (such as Ether).

The key idea of an LP is balance. The value on the token side should always match the value on the paired cryptocurrency side. This is called the 'LP equation' and is used to determine the price of the token, which is the value of the paired cryptocurrency in the LP divided by the number of tokens on the other side of the LP.

Decentralized exchanges (DEXs) are applications where users can buy and sell tokens. DEXs host and manage LPs, on which tokens can be 'swapped' for other coins and tokens, but not for fiat currencies. This is why, DEXs are sometimes informally called 'swaps'. Prominent examples of DEXs are Pancakeswap and Uniswap, which host LPs for a wide variety of tokens on the BNB Chain and Ethereum respectively.

'Automated Market Makers' (AMMs) are additional math-equations used by DEXs to govern the mechanics of their hosted LPs. The most popular AMM is the 'Constant Product Market Maker' (CPMM), an equation which forces the product of the number of cryptocurrency tokens/coins on the two sides of the LP to be a positive constant.

On a DEX, users can interact with LPs to buy or sell tokens. When buying a token, users deposit a desired amount of the paired cryptocurrency into the respective side of its LP and take out tokens from the other side, which increases the token's price. Conversely, when selling the token, users deposit a desired number of the tokens into the LP and withdraw some of the paired cryptocurrency, thereby decreasing the token's price. This seamless mechanism allows for fluid exchange dynamics reflecting real-time shifts in supply and demand.

When users interact with LPs to buy or sell tokens, they need to pay a 'liquidity provider fee' in addition to the gas fee. This fee is proportionally paid out to all liquidity providers based on their share of the LP. Liquidity providers include the internal DEX team, and more broadly consist of multiple external participants who provide liquidity through openly accessible platforms hosted by the DEX. This minimizes centralization risks by allowing anyone to contribute liquidity and earn proportionate fees.

AMMs like CPMM, at first glance, seem like an unnecessary addition to the mechanics here, but they are required to ensure that neither side of an LP can ever be completely emptied out (or made to zero) through buying or selling, since their product must be maintained at the CPMM constant which is a positive number. This leads to some interesting consequences such as 'slippage'.

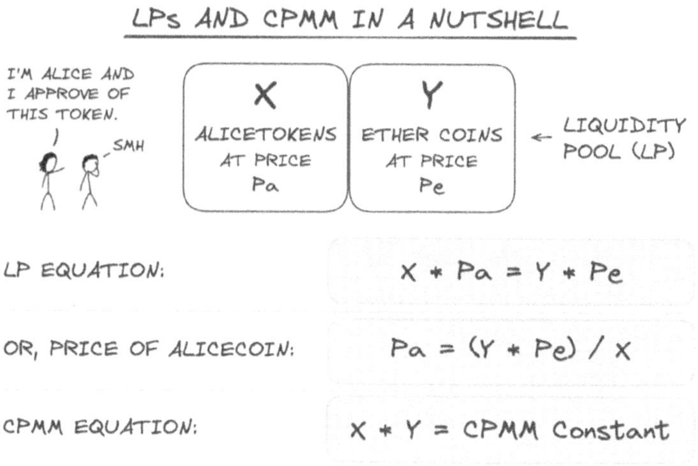

Let's understand the mechanics at play here with an example. Consider an LP with 10 'Alicetokens' on one side and 5 Ether coins (let's use the short form – 'ETH') on the other, with the market price of ETH at 4,000$.

Using the LP equation, the value of the 10 Alicetokens in the LP should be the same as the value of the 5 ETH on the other side of the LP. Or…

Hence, the price of Alicetoken in this situation will be...

Now, let's assume that you have 5 ETH (which are worth 5*4,000$=20,000$). Since your ETH holdings are exactly worth the 10 Alicetokens in the LP, you should be able to buy all 10 Alicetokens from the LP, right? Wrong, since that would empty out the Alicetoken side of the LP, and the CPMM won't allow this.

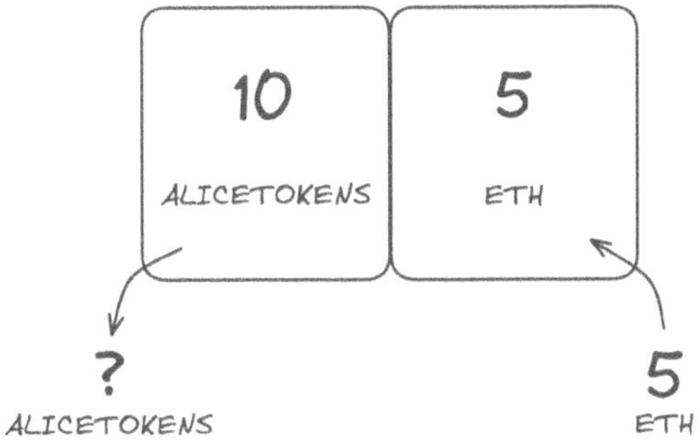

So, how many Alicetokens can you buy out of this LP for your 5 ETH? Well, first, let's calculate the CPMM constant for this LP. That would be...

With your buy order, you basically deposit 5 ETH into the corresponding side of the LP. So, now this side of the LP has 10 ETH (5 from before + 5 new ones you put in). The CPMM constant still needs to be maintained at 50. So, the new number of Alicetokens in the LP should be...

So, 5 Alicetokens must remain in the LP out of the initial 10. Which means, you get only the balance 5 Alicetokens through this transaction, instead of the 10 that you expected based on the initial price of

Alicetokens alone. The loss that you incurred is 50%, which is the 'slippage' of your transaction.

The new price of an Alicetoken after the transaction is completed will be...

...which is a 300% increase from its price before the buy order was executed. This change is called 'price impact' of the transaction.

Please note, what we covered here represents the predominant price determination mechanism used by most tokens in operation today. However, the space is evolving rapidly, with a wide variety of other models being implemented across numerous DEXs. For instance, there are some novel mechanisms that don't use LPs at all, but rather leverage minting and burning of tokens to match demand and supply. The price determination in these mechanisms differs from what we covered, but most of them still use ratio mechanisms like in LPs for calculating token prices.

Additionally, smart contracts of many tokens impose more conditions on how a token can be bought, sold, or transferred. For instance, some tokens have a buy and sell tax, which means the token's developers take some percentage of the amount involved when the token is bought or sold.

Popular tokens can also be listed on CEXs, where their prices are determined by the same order book mechanism which we discussed for coins. These prices are then balanced across multiple DEXs and CEXs using arbitrage.

Arbitrage

Many cryptocurrencies are listed on multiple CEXs and DEXs, each one determining their price independently using order books or LPs. The price of a cryptocurrency is continuously balanced across all CEXs and DEXs listing it, through arbitrage.

Arbitrage, in this context, is the practice of capitalizing on price differences of a cryptocurrency across different CEXs/DEXs. Traders buy it in a CEX/DEX where it's cheaper and sell it in another where it's priced higher, earning a profit from the price difference. As they do this, they naturally drive the price up in the cheaper CEX/DEX due to increased buying and drive it down in the pricier CEX/DEX because of increased selling. This activity tends to balance out prices across CEXs/DEXs, making them more consistent.

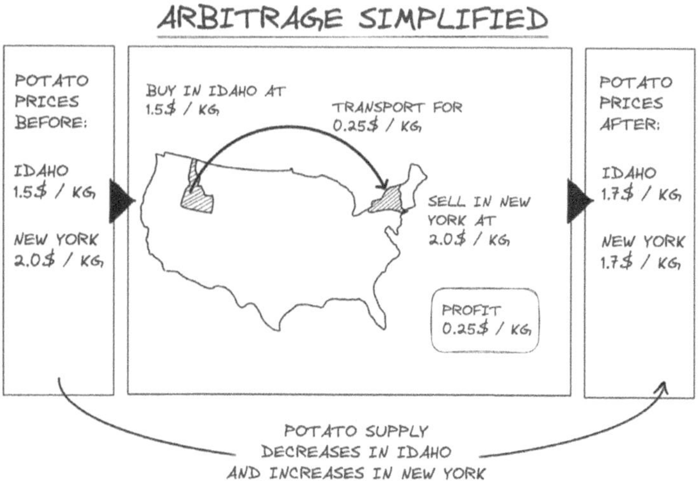

In the world of cryptocurrencies, arbitrage can be difficult to execute smoothly due to factors like varying transfer times, transaction fees, and rapidly changing prices. Nonetheless it's an important element, constantly ensuring that the prices of cryptocurrencies are quickly leveled out between markets.

Aside from price, two other common metrics to valuate cryptocurrencies are their 'market capitalization' (or 'market cap') and 'liquidity'.

The 'market cap' of a cryptocurrency is the product of its price and its circulating supply. The circulating supply of a cryptocurrency is the total number of its coins or tokens that are currently in circulation. For instance, Bitcoin's circulating supply at the time of writing (March 2024) is ~19.65 million Bitcoins, and it's price is ~65,000$, which puts its market cap at ~1.27 trillion$. But this does not mean that there are actually 1.27 trillion$ of fiat money in Bitcoin markets. That's where liquidity comes into the picture.

'Liquidity' of a cryptocurrency means the ease of buying and selling it. Liquidity is quantified as the value of the funds or assets backing a cryptocurrency in its markets, for instance in its LPs or its order books. A large market cap is a desired characteristic, but is meaningless in the absence of sufficient liquidity. For instance, a token can have a large market cap due to a high circulating supply, but very small LPs which make it difficult to buy or sell without taking massive slippages.

The demand for cryptocurrencies is significantly influenced by public perception, which can change swiftly due to their speculative nature and relatively light regulatory oversight. Consequently, the rate at which fiat money is invested into and withdrawn from cryptocurrency markets (buying and selling cryptocurrencies) is quite high. If the size of the buy or sell orders for a cryptocurrency is comparable to (or greater than) the size of the quantified liquidity backing it, the price of the token is very volatile, or subject to swift and dramatic fluctuations. This is perfectly demonstrated by the Alicetoken example we went through earlier, where the price of Alicetoken went up by 300% through just one buy order that was the same size as the liquidity in its LP.

So, the next time you hear that Bitcoin's price is scaling new "all-time high" (ATH), or that the price of Dogecoin has unexpectedly "mooned" because of a Tweet Elon Musk put out, you know what's happening behind the scenes!

15.

STABLECOINS: BRIDGING CRYPTO TO TRADITIONAL ECONOMIES

The volatile nature of most cryptocurrencies, with prices often swinging dramatically over short periods, has been a concern for both investors and potential adopters. While these price fluctuations offer skilled traders avenues for significant returns, they can also pose challenges in using cryptocurrencies for day-to-day transactions. Stablecoins are the category of cryptocurrencies aiming to alleviate the downsides of volatility.

Stablecoins are cryptocurrencies designed to maintain a stable value by pegging them to a reserve or a reference point, most commonly fiat currencies like the US Dollar or the Euro. By doing so, they attempt to offer the best of both worlds: the decentralized and efficient nature of cryptocurrencies combined with the relative stability of fiat currencies.

Stablecoins are classified based on the mechanisms they use to maintain their pegs to the respective fiat currencies. There are two broad types of stablecoins: collateralized and algorithmic.

Collateralized stablecoins are backed by a reserve of fiat currency at a 1:1 ratio. The idea is simple: for each unit of stablecoin minted and put into circulation, an equivalent unit of fiat currency is held in reserve. When these stablecoins are sold back to the issuer, they are burned, and the corresponding amount of fiat currency comes out of this reserve. Tether and TrueUSD are examples of collaterized stablecoins.

Algorithmic stablecoins are not backed by any collateral, but rather make use of algorithms to remain pegged. These algorithms are usually executed by smart contracts and automatically adjust the supply of the stablecoin aiming to match demand and maintain stability. Some algorithmic stablecoins also integrate repositories of other cryptocurrencies in their smart contracts and leverage their value to aid in stabilizing the peg, though these repositories do not serve as direct collateral in the conventional sense. Ampleforth and DAI are examples of algorithmic stablecoins.

Due to their price-stability, stablecoins serve as a bridge between cryptocurrencies and traditional financial systems. Usually investors convert their local (fiat) currencies into stablecoins, and then use these stablecoins to buy other cryptocurrencies. Vice versa, investors also sell their cryptocurrencies for stablecoins, and then convert these stablecoins into fiat currencies. In crypto-speak, these actions are respectively called 'on-ramping' and 'off-ramping' between fiat currencies and cryptocurrencies, and are usually done on centralized exchanges (CEXs).

Additionally, stablecoins provide a means for protecting the value of cryptocurrency investments from market fluctuations. Investors frequently convert their cryptocurrencies into stablecoins as a precautionary measure during periods of unpredictable market behavior, this strategy insulates the investment's worth from the volatility of cryptocurrency prices. The steady value of stablecoins also makes them ideal for transactions, safeguarding against the rapid price changes common in other cryptocurrencies.

Stablecoins are a cornerstone in the rapidly growing decentralized finance (DeFi) sector, serving as stable mediums for various financial activities like lending, borrowing, and earning interest. They also enable quicker and more cost-effective international transactions than traditional banking systems.

Despite these paramount roles, stablecoins have often faced challenges related to their trustworthiness and credibility. Though pegged, they operate in a decentralized manner and are not backed by the issuing authorities of their fiat counterparts. So, trust remains paramount, as users need to be confident that issuers genuinely maintain the necessary collaterals or the robustness of algorithms to maintain their stablecoins' pegs.

Sometimes stablecoins lose their pegs and trade below their fiat counterparts' values. This can happen due to insufficient, volatile, or illiquid collaterals to match market demand in case of collateralized stablecoins, and algorithm-failures beyond workable thresholds in case of algorithmic stablecoins.

Notably, algorithmic stablecoins have demonstrated a particular vulnerability with several instances of failure, underscoring the complexities inherent in maintaining stability without tangible collaterals. The death-spiral of Terra USD in 2022 is the most significant example.

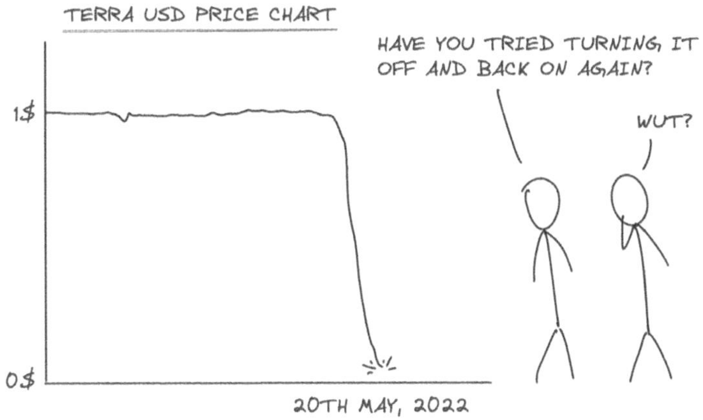

Given these challenges, there's an increasing push for regulatory oversight around stablecoins, e.g., tighter requirements of transparency around collaterals. This is a good thing, since with the necessary regulations in place, stablecoins' significance will likely grow, further connecting the crypto and traditional financial landscapes.

Speaking of regulation, how about governments leverage the benefits of blockchain technology and issue their own stablecoins? Well, in a way, they are starting to do so by officially issuing Central Bank Digital Currencies (CBDCs). These are like stablecoins, issued by the same authority as a country's currency, and pegged to that currency. Although, I hesitate to call CBDCs 'stablecoins' or even 'cryptocurrencies', because although they operate on blockchains (or other similar forms of distributed ledgers), they are extremely centralized which is against the core premise of blockchain technology. As the global economy becomes increasingly digitized,

CBDCs will likely play a pivotal role in shaping the future of money and commerce. However, a careful and collaborative approach, balancing innovation with regulation, will be crucial to their long-term success and acceptance.

16.

ANATOMY OF INITIAL COIN OFFERINGS (ICOs)

One of the first challenges start-ups face is raising funds to kick-start operations. Traditional ways to raise funds include seeking angel investments, venture capital, and bank loans. Each of these methods comes with its own challenges. For example, venture capital might demand disproportionate equity in the company, diluting the founder's ownership, and bank loans might bring unwanted debt and interest.

Initial Coin Offerings (ICOs) are a new form of fundraising that has emerged with the proliferation of blockchain technology and cryptocurrencies. Unlike traditional fundraising methods, ICOs have provided startups, especially those in the blockchain and cryptocurrency sectors, with a quicker and sometimes less regulated way to raise substantial amounts of money.

In raw terms, ICO is a crowdfunding mechanism leveraging cryptocurrency token sales. During an ICO, rather than selling shares like in an Initial Public Offering (IPO), a company issues newly created cryptocurrency tokens to investors at a fixed price per token for a limited period, usually charged in established cryptocurrencies like Bitcoin or Ether. ICOs can vary in their accessibility – some may be exclusively by invitation, allowing only select groups of investors to participate, while others are open to the public, permitting any interested individual to invest.

ICOs are sometimes referred to as 'token pre-sales'. Tokens don't typically signify company ownership or access to dividends in the way shares do, but instead offer specific current or future benefits within the company's ecosystem, such as access to services, products, or network participation. Investors are drawn to ICOs not just for these utilities but also in the hope that, as the company prospers, so will the token price.

HOW AN ICO WORKS - SIMPLIFIED EXAMPLE

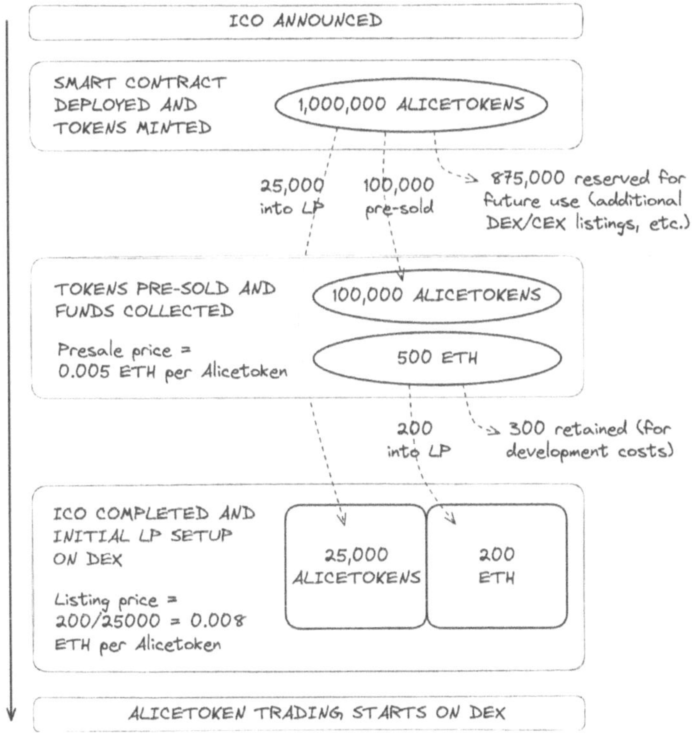

After an ICO is completed, the company makes the token available for open trading. Usually, trading is opened on DEXs using LPs first, at an equal or higher price than the pre-sale. It eventually lists and trades on CEXs if and when the company becomes established enough (since most CEXs have minimum daily trading volume requirements and additionally charge hefty premiums to list tokens).

ICOs have transformed the way start-ups in the blockchain space gather capital, by providing platforms for disruptive, often groundbreaking ideas to secure funding, and have fast-tracked numerous innovative blockchain technologies. They have also gathered a lot of buzz, as in certain instances, early ICO investors reaped staggering returns, purchasing tokens for pennies that later appreciated manifold.

The most prominent example of an ICO is Ethereum itself. In July-September 2014, this ICO sold Ethers at a price of 0.3-0.4$ each, in Bitcoin, and raised around 16 million$. These funds were then used for developing the Ethereum blockchain, for which the pre-sold Ether became the native coin. Ethereum, with its innovative smart contract capabilities, has since emerged as one of the preferred platforms for conducting ICOs.

ICOs come with their own risks, though. The decentralization that is core to ICOs, while being their strength, is also a vulnerability. The buzz they generate attracts a lot of investors, and, inevitably, bad actors. There have been numerous regrettable episodes where unscrupulous individuals vanished post-fundraising, leaving investors bereft.

Furthermore, after the ICO, when the token is available to trade on DEXs, it is subject to wild price fluctuations if the liquidity pool is small in value. Also, as mentioned earlier, unlike traditional investments, ICO tokens rarely grant ownership rights, leaving investors with minimal recourse if a project capsizes.

For these reasons, ICOs are often under regulators' microscopes. These regulations don't yet have any structure or uniformity to them, and the global landscape is a patchwork of responses with some nations embracing ICOs without any restrictions, others prohibiting them, and yet others requiring them to be registered as securities. Regulating ICOs more uniformly and strictly might help to mitigate some of the issues around them and amplify many of their benefits.

WEB3

17.

LET'S TALK WEB3: THE NEW ERA OF THE INTERNET

In the last three and a half decades, the internet has profoundly reshaped our world, transforming how we communicate, learn, work, transact and entertain ourselves. The story of the internet is one of continuous evolution and transformation.

The first decade and a half of the internet, called 'Web1', was marked by static web pages that acted like digital brochures. Websites during this era were read-only, with users consuming content rather than interacting with it. Examples from this period include the early versions of Yahoo, the AltaVista search engine, and the GeoCities web hosting service. These platforms offered a revolutionary way to quickly access information but had very limited two-way interactions.

The next era, called 'Web2', came in the mid-2000s and ushered in a more dynamic and interactive internet. This era is characterized by the rise of social media platforms like Facebook and Twitter (now X), e-commerce giants like Amazon and eBay, and user-generated content hubs like YouTube. Unlike Web1, the internet is no longer just a passive read-only medium. Users can create profiles, post updates, share photos, write blogs, and even sell products online. Collaboration tools like Zoom and Dropbox allow real-time co-working, and platforms like Instagram and TikTok have transformed personal branding and digital storytelling.

In Web2, control over all content and data is still centralized over a handful of tech corporations. Though you can still technically 'own' assets on Web2, like photos on your Facebook page, they are in these corporations' custody and not yours, same way as your money is in your bank's custody and not yours.

That's what the next era of the internet, 'Web3', aims to change. **Web3, which is emerging with the advent of blockchain technology, represents a migration of the internet towards decentralized ecosystems** where access and ownership are controlled by the community instead of a few large corporations. In Web3, in addition to reading and writing on the internet (like in Web1 and Web2), users can also truly own assets on the internet through tokenization powered by innovations such as non-fungible tokens (NFTs). Web3 also introduces the concepts of decentralized finance (DeFi) which provides financial services through smart contracts without traditional intermediaries, and decentralized autonomous organizations (DAOs), which are organizations run through rules encoded as computer programs on blockchains, eliminating the need for traditional hierarchical management.

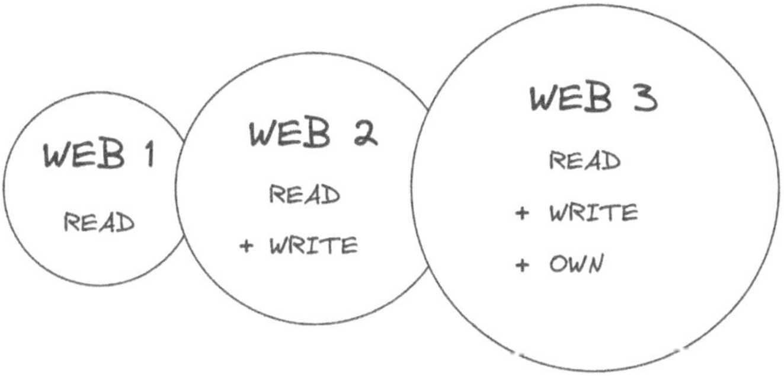

Web3 is still in its infancy and several wrinkles need to be ironed out before it is truly adopted at-scale, such as scalability, regulation, and sustainability.

One of the most pressing concerns for many blockchain networks underpinning Web3 is scalability.

Current leading blockchain platforms can handle only a limited number of transactions per second. As these platforms grow in popularity, they often face congestion, leading to slower transaction times and higher fees. Solutions like layer-2 scaling, sharding, and other blockchain architectures are being developed, but they're not adopted universally yet.

Web3, like any new disruptive technology, faces regulatory challenges. Governments worldwide are still figuring out how to regulate cryptocurrencies, ICOs, DeFi platforms, and other blockchain-based innovations. Regulatory ambiguity can deter institutional investors and businesses from entering the space.

Web3 will also not be adopted at scale unless blockchain technology becomes more sustainable. Proof-of-Work (PoW) blockchains, most notably Bitcoin, are often criticized for their high energy consumption. The PoW consensus mechanism requires vast amounts of computational power, leading to concerns about its environmental impact. Alternatives like Proof-of-Stake (PoS) and hybrid models are being preferred over PoW to mitigate this issue, but they come with risks of potential centralization which is against the ethos of Web3.

Despite these challenges, the potential of Web3 is monumental. Envision a digital realm where data privacy is restored, middlemen are eliminated, and users reap direct and immediate rewards from their online activities. As this new era unfolds, Web3 might just redefine the very fabric of the internet, ushering in a more equitable and transparent online world.

18.

DECENTRALIZED APPLICATIONS (DAPPS): A NEW BREED OF APPS

Applications, or ‘apps’, are software solutions designed to perform specific tasks or functions for users. After the internet became interactive in the era of Web2, apps emerged as platforms where users could interact with it. Today, it is hard to imagine our life without apps, such as messaging apps like WhatsApp, web browser apps like Chrome, social media apps like Twitter (now X), and service apps like Uber. Interactive web pages also fall under this category, e.g., Facebook. All these apps operate under centralized authorities (typically tech corporations) that control their data, functionality, and overall operation.

With the advent of Web3, a new type of apps is emerging: Decentralized applications, (DApps), which are powered by blockchain technology. Before we dive into the anatomy of DApps, you might want to quickly revise chapter 7 on smart contracts if you feel the need to jog your memory. Go do that first.

The core functionalities of DApps are conducted on blockchains primarily through smart contracts, which as you know are autonomous agreements enforced through snippets of code. These smart contracts are plugged into user interfaces (UIs) that look and feel like traditional apps (or web pages). Users interact with the smart contracts through these UIs using specialized connection tools, such as MetaMask or WalletConnect. These tools, which market themselves as gateways into the decentralized web, enable users to connect their blockchain accounts with these smart contracts through DApps, using their private keys (seed phrases) for authentication.

While interacting with the smart contract, the action initiation happens on the conventional UI or web interface, and the blockchain handles the core operations – especially all mechanisms governing trust, ownership, and transactions – in a decentralized manner. This allows DApps to offer the usability of traditional apps with the trust and transparency of decentralized systems.

All the essential data required to run DApps isn't typically stored on blockchains due to cost and speed considerations. Instead, it might be stored off-chain, or in decentralized storage systems like token-curated registries (TCRs) and the InterPlanetary File System (IPFS). TCRs are project-specific databases with entries that are maintained and curated by token holders, based on their vested interest in the quality and accuracy of the data. IPFS is a protocol designed to create a peer-to-peer method of storing and sharing data in a distributed file system. Unlike the traditional HTTP/HTTPS protocols, where your browser requests data from central servers, IPFS retrieves data from multiple locations.

Examples of popular DApps include decentralized finance (DeFi) platforms such as Aave and Compound which allow users to lend and borrow cryptocurrencies at algorithmically determined rates, blockchain games such as CryptoKitties and Star Atlas where players use NFTs as in-game resources, and decentralized exchanges (DEXs) like Pancakeswap and Uniswap where users can trade (swap) cryptocurrencies without centralized intermediaries. Speaking of DEXs, it's worth mentioning that centralized exchanges (CEXs) don't typically fall under the category of DApps, but rather work as traditional centralized apps, like your banking apps.

DApps mark a significant shift towards user empowerment and transparency compared to centralized platforms and applications, but their widespread adoption is still in its early stages due to concerns about scalability, user experience, interoperability, and compliance.

Popular blockchains on which DApps are built have often encountered scalability hurdles, affecting the performance and efficiency of DApps. Initiatives like Ethereum 2.0 aim to improve on these aspects. DApps also often grapple with user experience challenges. The complexity of managing cryptographic keys or navigating intricate interfaces can be daunting for the average user.

Then there's the lack of universal interoperability, a DApp on one blockchain doesn't always have the easy means to seamlessly interact with another on a different blockchain. This barrier, however, is being addressed with the increasing setup of developer- and user-friendly interoperability solutions, such as 'bridges', between different blockchains.

Meanwhile, regulatory concerns over DApps, especially those in the decentralized finance (DeFi) sector, mean that developers need to be proactive in ensuring compliance. At times this becomes cumbersome, as massive pivots need to be implemented in DApps for them to stay current with ever-evolving regulations.

Despite these challenges, the potential of DApps is vast, and as Web3 matures, they are set to play a transformative role in shaping many novel and exciting utilities that haven't been possible with Web1 and Web2.

19.

DECENTRALIZING GOVERNANCE USING BLOCKCHAINS

Many traditional companies consider shareholder input in decision-making processes. Shareholders can exert their influence on decisions through voting mechanisms, where the power of each vote is proportional to the number of shares owned by the voter. This kind of a governance model aims to balance leadership direction with stakeholder input. But it's not always transparent, with decision-making often obscured by bureaucracy and insider-group influence.

With the advent of Web3, a new form of organizations called **'decentralized autonomous organizations' (DAOs) have adapted traditional shareholder driven governance models to cryptocurrency token-holder driven ones.** It's the same basic concept, but with tokens as the new 'shares', and with increased transparency driven by blockchain technology.

Each DAO issues its own tokens, which its participants must procure and hold. Like traditional shares, these tokens enable their holders to vote on decisions regarding the DAO. However, unlike traditional shares, these tokens also additionally have other use cases within the DAO's ecosystem, such as access to its products and services. Every token-holder gets a say in decisions proportional to the number of the tokens they hold. In this way, the decision-making process in a DAO becomes a collective community-effort.

The governance rules of a DAO are encoded in smart contracts, ensuring transparency and resilience. These smart contracts enable any token-holder to create proposals typically in the form of multiple-choice polls, on which all token-holders can vote, and each vote has a weightage proportional to the number of tokens held by the voter. This way, decision making in the DAO is not centralized to an individual like a CEO, but rather decentralized over all token-holders.

Decentralized governance in DAOs doesn't mean that token-holders can change whatever they want.

Topics that are core to the DAO's existence are off limits through built-in safeguards. For instance, creation of proposals on certain key topics might only be limited to the foundational team of the DAO, or to token-holders who have locked-up a very high threshold number of tokens on the DAO's protocols. Additionally, proposals about topics close to the vision and mission of the DAO might require a unanimous vote (100% votes on only one option) to succeed.

The mechanism of token-driven decentralized governance introduced by DAOs has numerous upsides, reflecting the democratic scenarios that people have always wanted from being part of organizations.

DAOs introduce a level of transparency previously unseen in most organizations. Since every action, transaction, and decision is recorded on the blockchain, token-holders have a clear view of the organization's workings. This level of scrutiny reduces the chances of fraud and corruption.

DAOs can also operate without geographical boundaries, allowing for truly global organizations where members from different parts of the world can collaborate and contribute to decision making through their token-holdings.

Additionally, DAOs foster innovation without being held back by undue processes. Traditional organizations often suffer from bureaucratic red tape that stifles creativity and innovation. In contrast, DAOs, with their decentralized nature, encourage diverse perspectives and solutions since token-holders have the power to formally suggest ideas though proposals.

There are still lingering concerns about security, legality, and regulation of DAOs, the most obvious issue being who should be held accountable for a DAOs decisions and how. Nonetheless their promise of democracy with transparency is attracting both forward-looking innovators and traditionalists, and in recent times, DAOs have gained traction across a variety of sectors. Initiatives in Web3 like crowdfunding projects, managing decentralized finance protocols, or even making collective decisions on art acquisitions are increasingly adopting the DAO mechanism of governance.

20.

INTEROPERABILITY IN WEB3: BRIDGING BLOCKCHAINS

Blockchain technology is central to Web3's promise of a vast array of decentralized applications (DApps). However, there are hundreds of blockchains operational today, and the vision of a seamlessly connected Web3 requires their harmonious co-existence.

The diverse array of blockchains available today have been developed with specific use-cases and advantages in mind. For instance, while Ethereum might be celebrated for its pioneering smart contract capabilities, BNB Chain is preferred for its transaction efficiency and low gas fees. However, for a user or developer, this diversity in the absence of interoperability can be limiting. It's akin to having multiple isolated internet networks instead of one global internet.

Interoperability in the context of Web3 means enabling blockchains to seamlessly interact with each other without intermediaries. These cross-chain interactions can be simple data transfers or complex transactions involving cryptocurrencies. For instance, interoperability would enable a user on Ethereum to pay another user on BNB Chain, without having to switch blockchains or use third-party services or platforms.

Achieving this level of integration is not easy. Different blockchains operate on different consensus mechanisms, have distinct architectural designs, and use varying cryptographic techniques. Overcoming these differences requires sophisticated protocols that can understand and translate information across blockchains. Numerous Web3 projects are focused on solving this problem, through various interoperability solutions for cross-chain data transfers and cross-chain transactions.

Cross-chain data transfers are usually done by relaying data between smart contracts on source and destination blockchains. For instance, a smart contract on a blockchain recording Baseball game scores and statistics can be programmed to relay specific data points to a smart contract on another blockchain hosting sports betting applications and fantasy leagues. This might involve cryptographically protecting data during communications to avoid interception and tampering.

Cross-chain data transfers can be leveraged to subsequently trigger autonomous actions or events. For instance, confirmation of completion of services on the source blockchain can be relayed through a cross-chain data transfer, which upon receipt can trigger payments on the destination blockchain in its native coin. Such autonomous sequences are made possible by smart contracts.

Cross-chain transactions, which involve sending cryptocurrencies across blockchains, are complex multi-step endeavors that are facilitated by cross-chain swaps and bridges.

A 'cross-chain swap' involves paying a cryptocurrency on the source blockchain and receiving the equivalent amount in a different cryptocurrency on the destination blockchain. These are generally managed by 'atomic swap protocols', which are peer-to-peer trading solutions on an intermediary platform (which means the essence of decentralization is diluted to an extent).

There are also smart contract-based solutions available for making cross-chain swaps, where you pay a smart contract on the source blockchain, which then sends a confirmation to another smart contract on the destination blockchain (using a cross-chain data transfer mechanism), and upon receipt of the confirmation this smart contract pays you the same value in a different cryptocurrency on the destination blockchain.

'Bridges' are mechanisms that transfer cryptocurrencies on a one-to-one basis between different blockchains. There are three types of bridges based on their architecture: 'lock-and-mint', 'burn-and-mint', and 'lock-and-unlock'.

Let's understand how these three types of bridges work through an example scenario: Alice is an active user on Ethereum, and she wants to send 10 'Alicetokens' to Bob, who uses BNB Chain. She wants to do this without having to switch over to BNB Chain, and also without making Bob switch over to Ethereum.

The first type of bridges is 'lock-and-mint'. With a lock-and-mint bridge, Alice would lock up 10 Alicetokens in a smart contract on Ethereum. This smart contract would then relay a message to another smart contract on BNB Chain, which would mint (or create) 10 'wrapped' Alicetokens, which are one-to-one equivalents of Alicetokens on Ethereum. These wrapped Alicetokens, or 'wAlicetokens' would then be sent to Bob's BNB Chain address.

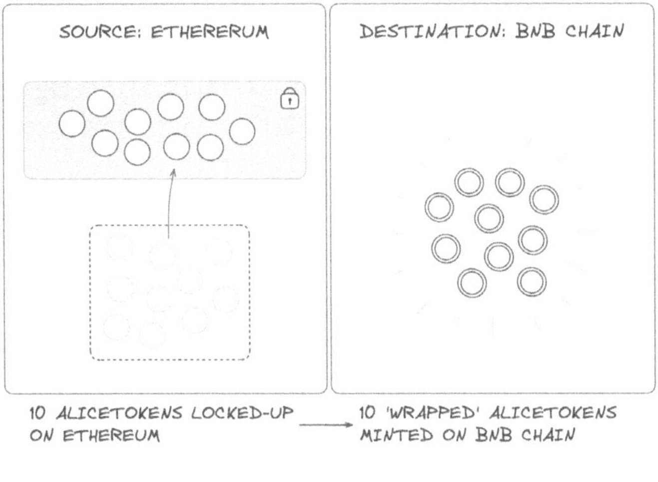

The second type of bridges is 'burn-and-mint'. With a burn-and-mint bridge, Alice would send 10 Alicetokens to a smart contract on Ethereum, which would burn (or destroy) them. It would then relay a message to another smart contract on BNB Chain, which would mint 10 wrapped Alicetokens and send them to Bob's BNB Chain address.

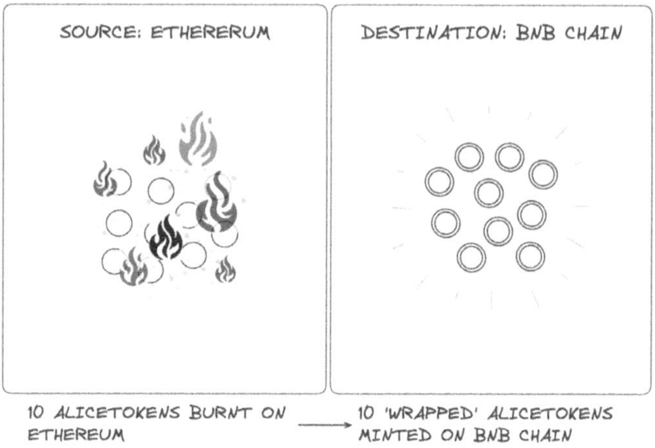

And lastly, the third type of bridges is 'lock-and-unlock'. On a lock-and-unlock bridge, Alice would lock up 10 Alicetokens in a smart contract on Ethereum. This smart contract would then relay a message to another smart contract on BNB Chain, which would unlock 10 wrapped Alicetokens from it.

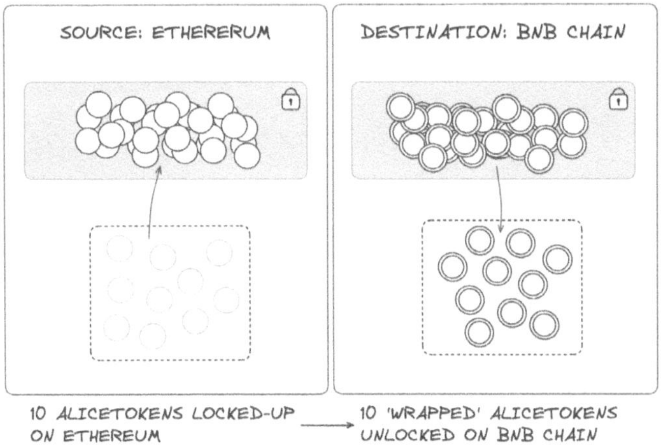

All three types of bridges ensure that the transfers of tokens are 'one-to-one', which means that the circulating Alicetoken supply (which excludes locked Alicetokens) across blockchains remains the same before and after each cross-chain transfer, thus preserving the token's value across blockchains.

All three types of bridges are also designed to be two-way, by running their underlying processes in reverse. For instance, in a lock-and-mint bridge, Bob can send 10 wrapped Alicetokens to the smart contract on BNB Chain, which would burn them and send a message to the smart contract on Ethereum, which in-turn would unlock 10 Alicetokens and send them to Alice's address.

As blockchains continue to specialize and proliferate across industries, the importance of creating robust, secure, and efficient interoperability solutions like bridges cannot be understated. Only with a truly interoperable Web3 can we hope to harness the full potential of decentralized technologies, enabling a more open, transparent, and inclusive digital future.

21.

NON-FUNGIBLE TOKENS (NFTS) AND THEIR APPLICATIONS IN WEB3

A Bitcoin is identical to another Bitcoin. This property is called 'fungibility'. If Alice and Bob exchange Bitcoins one-for-one, they will end up with the exact same thing as they had before.

However, not all cryptocurrencies operate this way. **Non-fungible tokens (NFTs) are a type of**

cryptocurrency tokens where each one is distinct and non-interchangeable, as the name suggests. Every NFT has a unique value and cannot be replaced with something else, unlike fungible tokens. This special quality makes NFTs perfect for digitally representing one-of-a-kind assets, including physical assets such as paintings, sculptures, real estate, vehicles, etc., and digital/intangible assets such as images, audios, videos, patents, copyrights, etc.

Note that due to this property, NFTs are often not directly classified under cryptocurrencies, but are rather known as 'cryptoassets'. In this book however, they have been classified under cryptocurrencies because despite being non-fungible, they share most of their other properties with cryptocurrency tokens.

An 'NFT collection' is a curated set of individual NFTs with common characteristics, themes, or branding. Each individual NFT within a collection remains unique with its specific properties which ensure its distinctness, but the overall grouping allows for thematic or artistic cohesion. Take the popular CryptoPunks NFT collection, for example. It features a series of character images, each with a unique appearance, yet all adhere to a common pixelated-art aesthetic. In the physical asset category, consider a luxury car brand that produces a limited series of 50 exclusive cars. The ownership of these cars could be sold as an NFT collection, in which each NFT would correspond to a specific car identified by unique features like registration number and original color.

But, all 50 NFTs in the collection would represent cars from the same limited series.

An NFT collection is issued by its creator(s) through its unique smart contract, like how fungible tokens are created. The address of this smart contract is often referred to as the 'contract address', or simply the 'contract' of the NFT collection. The smart contract determines the collection's rules and attributes, such as the maximum number of NFTs in the collection, the number of copies of each NFT available, etc. This setup is similar to how properties and rules of fungible tokens are managed through their own smart contracts.

The process of creating a new NFT within a collection is called 'NFT minting'. This process is governed by the NFT collection's smart contract. The process begins by creating a 'token ID', a unique identifier for the new NFT, which is crucial for distinguishing each NFT in the collection. The distinct properties of an NFT's underlying asset are linked to its token ID by encoding these properties into the NFT's metadata, which is then hashed and securely recorded on the blockchain alongside the token ID. For digital assets, these properties include its title, creator, creation date, description, and often a URL pointing to where the actual digital content is stored. For physical assets, properties might include specifics like the date, location, and seat number for a concert ticket.

The newly created token is then transferred to the minter's blockchain account address (unless the smart contract specifies differently). This involves cryptographic processes such as hashing, digital signing, and verification using the minter's private and public keys, as detailed in chapter 4. The ownership of the NFT can then be changed through trades or transfers on the blockchain following the rules defined in the smart contract of the NFT collection.

NFTs are most commonly minted, listed, and traded on special exchanges called 'NFT marketplaces'. These can be decentralized (like DEXs), where users hold the NFTs in their non-custodial blockchain accounts, and connect their accounts (via tools like Metamask and WalletConnect) to the NFT marketplace to transact. They can also be centralized (like CEXs), where custody of users' NFTs is with the owner of the marketplace, which users can access through their marketplace (not blockchain) accounts. OpenSea and NFTrade are popular examples of NFT marketplaces supporting creation and trading of NFT collections on multiple blockchains.

The pricing mechanisms for NFTs significantly differs from that of fungible cryptocurrencies. Unlike cryptocurrencies, whose prices are determined by order books, LPs and arbitrage, the prices of NFTs are set through more individualized methods such as listings on NFT marketplaces, auctions, or direct peer-to-peer transactions. This personalized approach to pricing reflects the unique characteristics and perceived value of each NFT, considering factors like rarity, demand, and the creator's reputation.

NFTs are being leveraged in several Web3 applications such as gaming, digital arts, physical collectables, event tickets, and more.

The gaming industry is a prominent example of NFT utility in Web3, transforming in-game assets into tradeable NFTs. Imagine games for which anyone can build unique resources (such as playable characters, skins, attires, weapons, lands, etc.), and sell them as NFTs. Or games where, upon achieving milestones, you get rare NFT badges to assert your reputation.

The Web3 gaming industry is also pioneering 'play to earn' and 'play to create' models, where players compete to earn in-game resources, buildable parts or even (fungible) cryptocurrency tokens. Popular games like Axie Infinity, Star Atlas, and Battle Leet are all examples of such games.

The art world has also been profoundly impacted by the emergence of NFTs, offering a ground-breaking method to authenticate, sell, and trade digital art. Beeple, a renowned digital artist, sold an NFT artwork titled "Everydays: The First 5000 Days" for a staggering 69 million$. Musicians like Grimes and 3LAU have sold multiple songs and soundtracks as NFTs, earning millions. These sales didn't just make news because of their high prices, but they underscored the transformative potential of NFTs in assuring the originality of a digital art piece. Unlike traditional art forms, which can be authenticated through physical examination and provenance, digital art can be easily copied, making its originality hard to prove. NFTs address this challenge by creating a verifiable digital certificate of authenticity on the blockchain.

Additionally, these NFTs representing artwork also give artists unprecedented control over their work. Artists can embed royalty mechanisms into their NFT smart contracts, ensuring they get a percentage of sales whenever one of their NFTs are resold. This is a significant shift from the traditional art market, where artists typically benefit only from the initial sale.

Rare physical assets have also been minted as NFTs to verify authenticity and ownership, although this is not as common yet as digital assets. For instance, Arianee is a project that has paired luxury watches with NFTs. By doing this, they ensure the authenticity of the watch and provide a tamper-proof record of its history and ownership.

Although NFTs specialize in signifying ownership to assets, fungible tokens can also be designed to serve similar utilities. 'Asset tokenization' is the broad process that converts real-world assets into tokens (fungible or non-fungible). Asset tokenization brings some interesting economic benefits and challenges, which we will discuss in chapter 28.

TECHNICAL CHALLENGES AND SOLUTIONS

22.

DECENTRALIZED ORACLES: CONNECTING BLOCKCHAINS TO THE REAL WORLD

Decentralized oracles are an integral yet often overlooked component of blockchain technology, acting as a vital link between blockchains and the external world. Simply put, **decentralized oracles enable blockchains, specifically smart contracts on blockchains, to securely interact with external data.**

Many smart contracts operate based on specific conditions and require precise and current real-world data to function effectively. Decentralized oracles meet this need by sourcing data from diverse external sources, processing it for accuracy, and integrating it seamlessly into the blockchain.

Take a smart contract running a Baseball Fantasy League, for instance. To distribute rewards, the contract requires up-to-date scores and player statistics from recent games. That's where a decentralized oracle comes in. It reliably sources this data, ensuring its accuracy and integrity, and feeds it into the smart contract. The smart contract then uses this data to calculate points scored by league participants and disburses rewards accordingly.

This process ensures a fair and transparent reward system, anchored in real-time sports data from the oracle.

Decentralized oracles rely on multiple independent data sources called 'oracle nodes' for ensuring data accuracy and reliability. An oracle node (not the same thing as a blockchain node) can be any external data source such as a website, database, server, or any other API. Having multiple oracle nodes feeding data helps prevent manipulation, bias, or inaccuracies.

For instance, for our Baseball Fantasy League smart contract that requires game scores, an oracle would not just look at one website or news report, it would scan several sources including official reports to determine the score in a reliable way. This would prevent participants manipulating data fed to the smart contract in their favour.

Decentralized oracles employ various mechanisms to verify the authenticity of the data they collect. This is one of their most critical aspects, failing which would defeat their purpose. One common method is the use of algorithms where multiple neutral entities (e.g., blockchain nodes or users) must agree on the data received from oracle nodes before it is accepted and passed to smart contracts. This process is akin to cross-checking facts from different sources before drawing a conclusion. Another approach is the use of reputation systems, where the oracle nodes are rated based on their historical accuracy and reliability. The ones that consistently provide accurate data are given higher credibility and even rewarded in cryptocurrency. This system encourages oracle nodes to maintain high standards of truthfulness and accuracy.

Decentralized oracles also often make use of cryptographic techniques to ensure that the data remains tamper-proof during transmission. For instance, before transmitting data to the blockchain, an oracle node can generate a cryptographic hash of the data and digitally sign it (similar mechanism to the one discussed in chapter 4). Such security measures help protect the data from being altered by malicious actors before it reaches the intended smart contract.

As blockchain technology expands its relevance in various industries, the role of decentralized oracles is bound to be the "Robin to blockchains' Batman". Decentralized oracles will play vital roles in blockchain technology's proliferation across diverse industries, such as healthcare, supply chain management, renewable energy harnessing, environmental monitoring, and the metaverse. Afterall, blockchains are all about data, and decentralized oracles play an important part in providing that data securely.

23.

BLOCKCHAIN SCALABILITY ISSUES AND SOLUTIONS

One of the most significant technical hurdles blockchain technology has faced is **scalability, which is the ability to handle a large volume of transactions without succumbing to network congestion, increased transaction costs, or long processing times.**

Achieving scalability is essential for blockchain technology to fulfil its manifesto of decentralized global utility. This challenge is inherently tied to the design of many traditional blockchains, which prioritize security and decentralization. For instance, the Bitcoin blockchain can manage only about 7 transactions per second (tps), whereas traditional payment processors like Visa can handle over 25,000 tps. This discrepancy highlights a challenge facing blockchain technology in becoming a viable alternative for large-scale financial transactions.

To address these scalability issues, several solutions have been proposed and are in various stages of development. Let's use the analogy of a blockchain as a congested highway to understand these solutions.

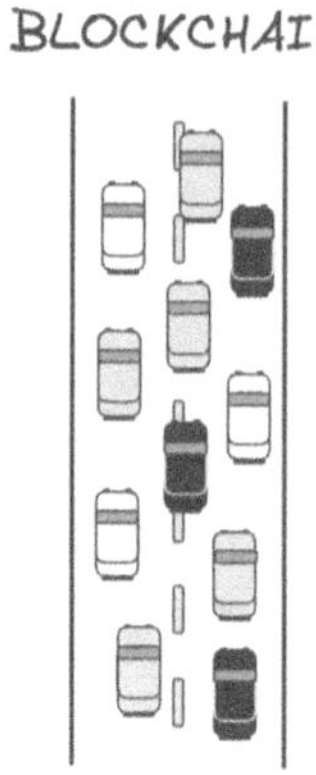

The first and most obvious solution to decongest our highway is to add more lanes to it. That would be the direct solution of **'on-chain scaling', which involves tweaking the original blockchain protocol itself to allow for more transactions per block** by increasing block sizes and/or reducing the time between blocks.

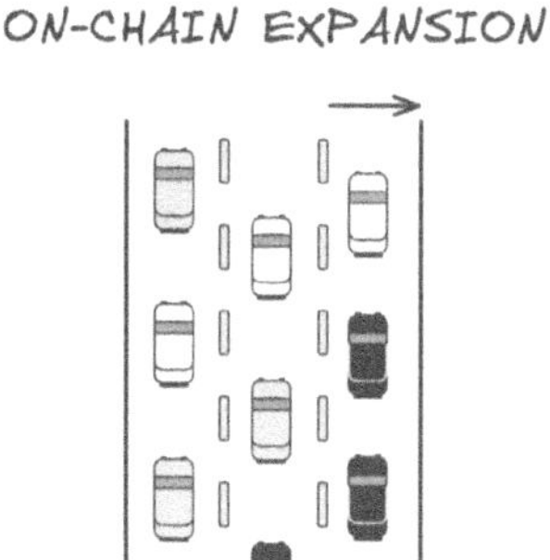

On chain scaling could potentially lead to centralization, as larger block sizes and lower block times require more computational power to process, potentially side-lining smaller node operators.

The second solution is to add a toll-discounted carpool lane along the main highway to incentivize people to pool and reduce the number of vehicles. This is the idea behind **'layer-2 solutions', which streamline transaction processing and reduce gas fees by aggregating (pooling) multiple transactions before collectively submitting them to the main chain.** For instance, the Lightening Network for Bitcoin creates a network of payment channels between users that facilitate instant, low-cost transactions without requiring immediate blockchain confirmation. Only the opening and closing of these channels are recorded on the blockchain, significantly reducing the transaction load on the main ledger.

LAYER-2 SOLUTIONS

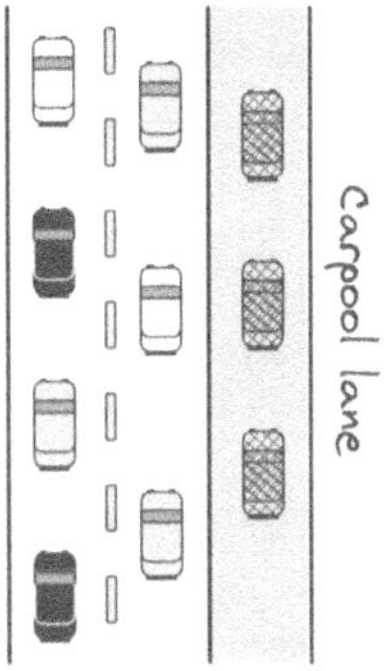

Layer-2 solutions enhance transaction throughput by leveraging the main blockchain's security, though they introduce complexity and risk centralization around specific technologies or operators. Visualize the potential inconvenience of driving on a carpool lane built and operated by a private company enforcing slightly different traffic rules and regulations than the rest of the public highway lanes.

The third solution is to add a parallel side-road connected to the highway at both ends, to take some vehicles off of it and decongest it. This is achieved by **'sidechains', which function as independent blockchains that are tethered to the main blockchain through two-way pegs (like bridges), enabling assets to move seamlessly between the two and facilitating efficient transaction offloading.** An example of a sidechain to Ethereum is Polygon, which was created to solve Ethereum's (pre-2.0) scalability issues by using a PoS consensus mechanism for faster and cheaper transactions. Polygon quickly became a preferred blockchain destination for developers and users alike, due to its scalability and user-friendly design.

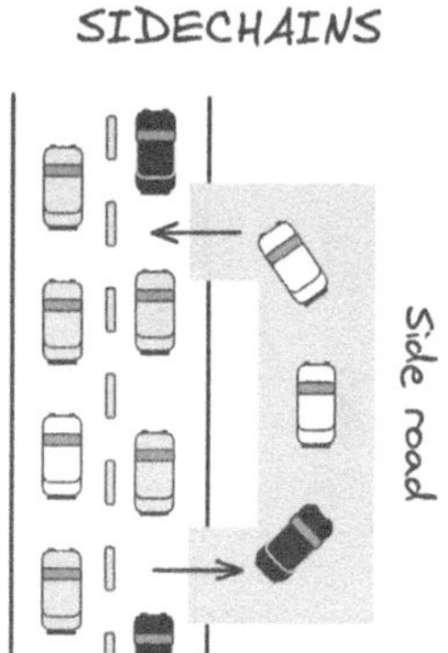

Sidechains offer scalability by taking assets and transactions off the main blockchain. However, there's a potential trade-off: this can compromise security and decentralization if the protocols used by the sidechain are not as robust as the ones used by the main blockchain. This is akin to a side-road not having the same level of structural integrity and oversight as the main highway.

Last but not the least, the fourth solution is to split the highway into multiple roads, one for each destination. This is the idea behind **'sharding', which partitions the blockchain into smaller, manageable 'shards', and each one processes a fraction of the total transaction load, enabling concurrent transaction processing.** One of the first successful implementations of sharding on a public blockchain was achieved by Zilliqa. Ethereum 2.0 is also implementing sharding (amongst other innovations) to significantly improve Ethereum's scalability.

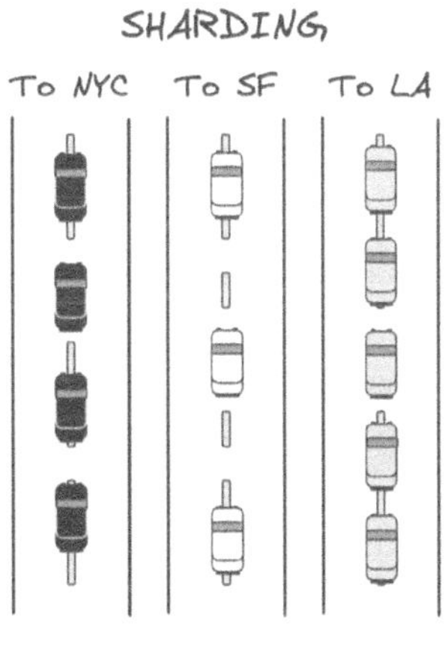

While sharding promises to boost transaction throughput to achieve scalability, it also complicates cross-shard transactions and the maintenance of blockchain's stringent security standards. Imagine a car heading south from Portland with one passenger getting dropped off in San Francisco and another going all the way to Los Angeles, and you'll see why separate highways to the two destinations would slightly complicate things for this trip.

In the end, each solution to the scalability challenge presents its own unique trade-offs between scalability, security, and decentralization. Nonetheless, combinations of these solutions implemented with efficient consensus mechanisms (such as PoS) and robust interoperability have proven to be very effective at scaling blockchain networks while maintaining security and decentralization. For instance, Ethereum 2.0 is leveraging a switch from PoW to PoS, along with scaling mechanisms such as sharding, to evolve Ethereum's capacity from ~30 tps to ~100,000 tps. As blockchain developers and the wider community continue to innovate, it is becoming clear that the scalability challenge is not insurmountable but rather a stepping stone on the path toward achieving widespread adoption of blockchain technology.

24.

PRIVACY ON BLOCKCHAINS: ZERO-KNOWLEDGE PROOFS AND MORE

Traditional blockchains, such as Bitcoin, are pseudo-anonymous (or pseudonymous), they mask identities with addresses but leave a transparent trail of transactions. In certain cases, patterns can be traced, compromising user privacy. With the adoption of blockchain technology across various industries, this has been a concern, especially for enterprises. Consequently, there's an increasing need for confidentiality alongside the benefits of a decentralized ledger.

The most extensively implemented solution to this need is the concept of zero-knowledge proofs. **A zero-knowledge proof (ZKP) is a cryptographic mechanism through which one party proves to another that a statement is true, without revealing any information beyond the validity of the statement itself.**

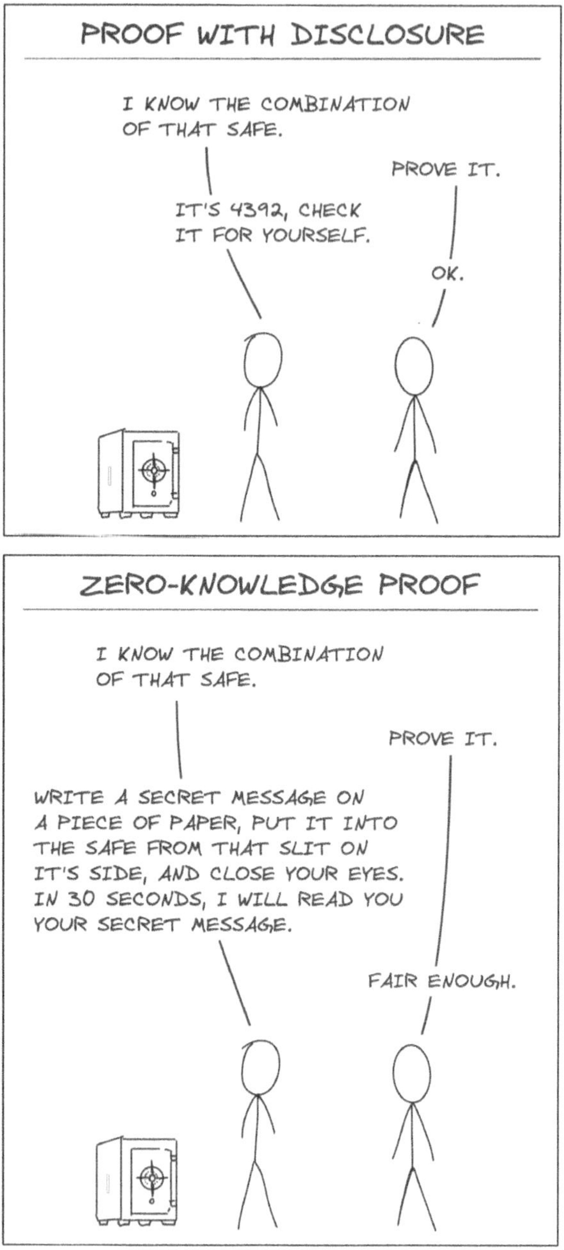
PROOF WITH DISCLOSURE
I KNOW THE COMBINATION OF THAT SAFE.
PROVE IT.
IT'S 4392, CHECK IT FOR YOURSELF.
OK.
ZERO-KNOWLEDGE PROOF
I KNOW THE COMBINATION OF THAT SAFE.
PROVE IT.
WRITE A SECRET MESSAGE ON A PIECE OF PAPER, PUT IT INTO THE SAFE FROM THAT SLIT ON IT'S SIDE, AND CLOSE YOUR EYES. IN 30 SECONDS, I WILL READ YOU YOUR SECRET MESSAGE.
FAIR ENOUGH.

Let's break down how ZKPs work in the context of blockchain transactions using, yet again, an example of Alice sending 10 'Alicetokens' to Bob.

But this time, it's on a blockchain that uses ZKPs for user privacy. Every such blockchain has a specific predefined ZKP process, which allows users to create cryptographic 'proofs' of their initiated transactions, without revealing their details such as their address to anyone including the blockchain's nodes. This process also allows nodes to verify the cryptographic proofs sent by users, without needing to see the actual transaction data.

Alice initiates the process by creating a cryptographic proof of the transaction message using this predefined process. This proof demonstrates Alice's ability to make the transaction to Bob, confirming that she owns 10 (or more) Alicetokens, without disclosing her or Bob's addresses.

She then broadcasts the transaction along with the proof to the blockchain's nodes, in such a way that the transaction details are not visible to the nodes, only the proof is. The nodes then verify the proof, confirming the transaction's validity.

Once verified, this transaction is added to a block, and then to the blockchain as per the consensus mechanism, without anyone seeing the actual details of the transactions in the block such as sender and receiver addresses. Once this is done, the ledger gets updated, Bob's balance increases by 10 and Alice's balance decreases by 10. This update is synchronized across the blockchain, maintaining an accurate and up-to-date record of all transactions.

The use of ZKPs enables both users and developers to selectively manage the visibility of information on the blockchain. Privacy frameworks can be customized, accommodating the diverse privacy requirements of various users and applications. While the blockchain ledger typically remains accessible to the public, allowing anyone to view active balances of each address, all details of transactions such as sender and receiver addresses can be concealed. This approach promotes a balance between transparency for trust and privacy for user discretion.

Blockchains like Zcash, Horizen, and Komodo have implemented ZKPs to create shielded transactions, which obscure sender, receiver, and transaction amount. The popularity of these blockchains reflects the market's demand for enhanced privacy.

Privacy isn't just a concern for cryptocurrency transactions. Smart contracts, which automate execution of agreements on blockchains when required conditions are met, also benefit from these features. Here, ZKPs can be used to verify the fulfilment of contract terms without revealing the specifics, opening avenues for blockchain application in sensitive domains like healthcare and finance where confidentiality is not a luxury, but a necessity.

Aside from ZKPs, other privacy-enhancing technologies are also making headway in the world of blockchains. For instance, Monero has introduced the concept of 'ring signatures', which involves using a private key to sign a transaction in a way that it's mixed with past transactions pulled from the blockchain to obscure transaction details. 'Homomorphic encryption' is another potential approach being considered by some upcoming blockchains. This approach enables computations on encrypted data, yielding encrypted results that, when decrypted, match the results of the same computations had they been conducted on the unencrypted data. This allows data to remain encrypted while being processed, offering a high degree of privacy and security.

Despite these advances, privacy solutions on blockchains face a lot of challenges. There's the question of balance between privacy and the regulatory requirements for transparency, particularly in combating fraud, money laundering, and financing of terrorism. The very features that make blockchains a haven for privacy enthusiasts can also make them attractive for illicit activities.

Furthermore, integrating advanced privacy-preserving techniques like ZKPs typically requires highly specialized knowledge and can introduce new complexities and inefficiencies into the blockchain. There's an ongoing need for optimization to ensure that these technologies do not excessively hamper transaction speeds or inflate costs.

As the blockchain community continues to grapple with these challenges, it's clear that the pursuit of privacy is not just about keeping secrets, it's about establishing a new paradigm of digital trust. Blockchains promise a world where we can interact and transact without surrendering the details of our lives to public gaze or compromising the security and integrity of our data, and these advanced privacy features like ZKPs bolster that promise.

25.

QUANTUM COMPUTING AND THE FUTURE OF BLOCKCHAINS

In chapter 4, we saw how public-key cryptography is used to secure blockchain transactions by encrypting (or, digitally signing) them. Let's take a closer look at the concepts of encryption and decryption, and how effective they really are for securing systems such as account access and transaction validity.

In general, **encryption is the process of converting readable data into a scrambled, unreadable format using a specific algorithm and (in most cases) a digital key, and decryption is the process reverting the scramble back to its original readable form.** Decryption requires the key that was used for encrypting the data, which is only supposed to be known to people who are authorized to access the data. If this key is unknown, the only alternative to access the data is to keep guessing until the correct key is found. This process is called 'breaking' or 'brute-forcing' the encryption.

Take the Caesar Cipher, for example. It encrypts text by shifting each letter a specified number of places in the alphabet. For instance, shifting "APPLE" by 1 changes it to "BQQMF", and by 4 to "ETTPI". Here, the numbers

1 and 4 act as keys. Given the English alphabet's 26 letters, a Caesar Cipher offers 26 possible keys. Without knowing the key, breaking this encryption could take up to 26 guesses. Not a big deal, is it? Most people can break that in a minute, but it still takes some amount of work (guessing) during that one minute!

That's the thing about encryption – it doesn't guarantee the security of data, it just makes it more difficult to get to the data by brute force, because you must guess the key, and this requires work. The better the encryption, more the work (number of guesses) required, hence more the computational power needed, and hence more the difficulty.

It's like putting a lock on your door. It doesn't guarantee that no one would break into your house, it just makes it difficult. The stronger the lock, the more the difficulty to break in.

With that in mind, let's go back to the example from chapter 4 where Alice sends 10 coins to Bob. Alice's digital signature, which is an encryption that she creates using her private key, enables the security and authenticity of the transaction. If Bob knows or guesses Alice's private key (or seed phrase), he could control her account by creating her digital signatures.

Luckily, private keys on blockchains operational today are not based on anything like the Cesar Cypher. They are typically at least 256 bits long, which means they are 256-digit binary numbers. Mathematically, there are 2^{256} different possible combinations for a 256-digit binary number. 2^{256} is a stupidly large number, it's actually orders of magnitude more than the number of atoms in our galaxy. If Bob tries guessing Alice's private key, even with the whole world's computing power at his disposal, it would take him an unimaginable amount of time – far beyond hundreds of thousands of years – to do that.

The only practical way for him to get control of Alice's account is to steal her private key or seed phrase. Brute force is not an option.

Unless, he has a quantum computer.

In a nutshell, **quantum computing leverages principles of quantum mechanics to perform complex calculations more efficiently than classical computing.** Quantum computers make this possible by using quantum bits, or 'qubits' as their building blocks. Unlike classical bits that can be either a 0 or a 1 at any particular point of time, qubits can exist in a state of 'superposition', where they are both 0 and 1 at the same time. They can also be 'entangled' with other qubits, a phenomenon that links particles no matter the distance separating them. Without getting too much into the physics of it, this enables quantum computers to process certain types of calculations exponentially faster than classical computers.

The integrity of most blockchains relies heavily on cryptographic algorithms like SHA-256, that are used to generate public-private key pairs and hash blocks. Current classical computers would take an unfathomable amount of time to brute-force these cryptographic systems. However, quantum computers bring to the table capabilities that could, in theory, easily unravel these systems, potentially exposing blockchains to the risk of fraud and theft.

So, if Bob had such a quantum computer, it could enable him to quickly decipher Alice's private key from her public key, which he could then use to control her blockchain account by digitally signing transactions from it.

As of now though, the idea of quantum computers breaking encryptions to unravel blockchains (or any other modern digital security systems) is more theoretical than practical. Current quantum computers are in their infancy, grappling with limitations in physical stability, qubit count, and error rates, which significantly restrict their ability to perform complex calculations required to challenge encryption methods like those used in blockchain technology. So, while the future might hold significant breakthroughs, today's encryption remains secure from the reach of quantum computing.

Even if, one day, quantum computing does get to the point of advancement to challenge cryptography, it also presents opportunities for cryptography to evolve. Just as quantum computing can break certain cryptographic algorithms, it can also help create quantum-resistant cryptography. These are encryption methods that could potentially be secure against the might of quantum computing. Blockchain networks can integrate these quantum-resistant algorithms to safeguard against future quantum threats.

Researchers and developers are actively exploring post-quantum cryptography to keep blockchain technology (and other technologies that rely on cryptography) one step ahead. This not only involves creating new algorithms but also ensuring that these quantum-proof solutions can be integrated into existing infrastructures seamlessly, without compromising their efficiency or scalability.

Quantum computing could also be the ultimate solution to blockchain scalability issues, as it can speed up complex calculations. These improvements could also make consensus mechanisms and smart contract execution more efficient, potentially revolutionizing advanced decentralized applications (DApps).

The advent of quantum computing is not all doom and gloom for cryptography. It's really a technological race where the finish line keeps moving as both fields advance.

ECONOMICS, SECURITY, AND REGULATION

26.

ECONOMIC PERSPECTIVES AROUND CRYPTOCURRENCIES

Although cryptocurrencies appear to have popped out of nowhere and taken the financial world by storm, **they have their roots in some long-standing economic theories around de-nationalization (or globalization) and scarcity of money.**

The inception of cryptocurrencies can be directly linked to the global disillusionment following the 2008 financial crisis, which was the spark that lit the fire. As traditional banking systems and financial institutions faltered, there arose a compelling need for a decentralized, transparent and 'trustless' monetary system free from central authority manipulation. Bitcoin, the first cryptocurrency, emerged in response, offering a new monetary paradigm.

Century-old ideas from the 'Austrian School of Economics' (which is a school of thought that focuses on spontaneous order arising from decentralized decisions), find resonance in this monetary paradigm. A prominent member economist-historian Ludwig von Mises, in his work "The Theory of Money and

Credit" (1912), introduced the 'regression theorem', attempting to explain the origin and value of money. He argued against the idea that money has intrinsic value and posited that the value of money is subjective, and dependent on its supply. **The value of money is not constant, and the more money central banks put in circulation, the less each unit of that money is worth – this phenomenon is called 'inflation'.**

Another member economist Friedrich Hayek expanded on these ideas and, in the mid-1970s, particularly in his book "Denationalisation of Money" (1976), argued for the abolition of the government's monopoly on the issuance of money. He believed that competition between private issuers would lead to better, more stable currencies.

Fiat currencies, like the US Dollar, are controlled by governments and can be printed in unlimited quantities by central banks that are affiliated to these governments, leading to potential inflation. Cryptocurrencies, on the other hand, aren't controlled by any central authorities and often have a predetermined supply, with timed releases defined in their underlying protocols. Bitcoin, for instance, has a supply cap of 21 million and the release of Bitcoins into the market is governed by robust mechanisms such as Bitcoin halving. These supply caps are designed to make cryptocurrencies inherently resistant to inflation.

Decentralization and scarcity of cryptocurrencies are design choices directly reflecting the Austrian School's critique against government control and limitless money printing leading to inflation. However, although these do seem like robust economic arguments in favor of cryptocurrencies, there are some daunting roadblocks in their intended path. Many of these roadblocks involve technology and security issues, but for the current chapter let's restrict ourselves to the economic roadblocks only.

Cryptocurrencies will probably never completely replace fiat currencies, because the latter have reached a pivotal threshold of social acceptance. And as long as that is true, 'value' will always be measured in fiat currencies. Consider this: If I were to ask you your monthly income, you'd be able to tell me the number in US Dollars (or your local fiat currency) instantly. But if I were to ask you your monthly income in Bitcoin, well you'd probably have to make some assumptions and calculations.

As the years have passed, cryptocurrencies have taken root more as an asset class (or an investment vehicle) than as currencies, which is probably not what Satoshi Nakamoto had in mind, going by his "peer-to-peer electronic cash system" whitepaper. And like any other asset class, they are not generally used as a unit of measuring value. Rather, their own value is measured in fiat currencies, which are the socially accepted units of value.

Tactically, this means that cryptocurrency prices are underpinned by fiat currencies through mechanisms such as order books (recall chapter 14). Such a system driven by fiat currencies leads to price volatility in cryptocurrencies, especially when the velocity of fiat money flowing in and out of cryptocurrency markets is high. Price volatility, or let's call it 'perceived value volatility' in this context, significantly hinders cryptocurrencies' potential as mediums of exchange. Furthermore, this volatility severely undermines their designed inflation resistance, and can also rapidly alter wealth distribution and consumption patterns, which can have undesirable effects on the economy.

Nevertheless, there have been several experiments all over the world, that have tried to integrate cryptocurrencies (mostly Bitcoin) as alternative currencies in traditional financial systems. For instance, El Salvador made Bitcoin an alternate legal tender alongside the US Dollar in 2021.

Such experiments have been hotly debated and widely opposed due to their potential for economic destabilization. In addition to the effects of volatility, critics argue that cryptocurrencies have the potential to drain an economy's currency reserves through seamless cross-border transactions. Additionally, the decentralized and less-regulated nature of cryptocurrencies makes them susceptible to market manipulations, fraud, and illicit activities, which can further erode economic stability.

As the conversation around cryptocurrencies progresses, it's evident that their path is marked by both potential economic benefits and downsides. Navigating the delicate balance between leveraging these advantages and mitigating the inherent risks is crucial. This equilibrium will significantly influence the future role of cryptocurrencies, determining whether they become widely accepted as currencies, assets, or a balanced hybrid of both – only time will tell.

27.

DECENTRALIZED FINANCE (DEFI): A NEW FINANCIAL PARADIGM

Decentralized finance (DeFi) refers to a financial ecosystem that operates without traditional financial intermediaries such as banks or brokerages. By leveraging blockchain technology, DeFi platforms allow users to participate in a slew of financial activities without being forced to navigate conventional financial middle-men or institutions.

The crux of DeFi lies in the ecosystem's open-source and permissionless nature. In traditional finance, centralized institutions act as gatekeepers, determining who can access financial services and under what specific terms. DeFi, on the other hand, allows anyone with an internet connection to access financial tools and services under transparent and universally impartial terms coded directly into smart contracts or blockchain protocols.

By democratizing finance in this way, DeFi holds the promise of leveling the financial playing field. It not only opens financial services to a wider audience but also targets the inclusion of the 'unbanked' and 'underbanked' – terms coined within the DeFi community to describe individuals sidelined by traditional finance.

Smart contracts serve as the backbone of DeFi. As you know, smart contracts live on blockchains and incorporate agreement terms directly into code, enabling transactions and agreements to be executed autonomously without the need for intermediaries. The DeFi landscape has expanded significantly in the past few years, offering smart contract-based alternatives for a vast array of traditional financial activities. An illustration of this is the scenario that we discussed in chapter 7 in which Alice rents Bob's apartment, which showcases how DeFi can revolutionize everyday transactions using smart contracts.

DeFi has introduced innovative models of generating returns on investments, such as yield farming and staking. These are very different from the interest models in traditional finance. Yield-farming enables users to earn rewards by lending their cryptocurrency holdings to liquidity pools (LPs). By participating in yield-farming, users essentially get rewarded by helping to increase the liquidity of the market, which in turn leads to more stable pricing of the cryptocurrencies involved. Staking enables users to lock up (or stake) cryptocurrencies to support the operation of a PoS blockchain network in exchange for rewards. These return-generating models have proven especially attractive to users in low-interest environments, as they often offer considerably higher returns than traditional investments, but at the risk of cryptocurrency price volatility.

Several DeFi platforms also offer novel lending, borrowing, and trading mechanisms using cryptocurrencies. For instance, 'flash loans' are smart contract driven mechanisms that allow users to borrow cryptocurrency without collateral, on the condition that the loan is repaid within the same block on the blockchain. If not repaid within the same block, the transaction reverses as if it never happened. Fees from these loans are distributed to the liquidity providers of the flash loan service. Flash loans are often leveraged for self-liquidation and arbitrage execution purposes.

DeFi also provides decentralized solutions for representing ownership of both physical and digital/intangible assets through a process known as 'asset tokenization'. This is achieved not only with non-fungible tokens (NFTs), which are unique digital certificates of ownership, but also with fungible tokens, which represent equal parts of a whole. We'll discuss asset tokenization in detail in the next chapter.

Lately, there have even been attempts to integrate DeFi into traditional finance. For instance, traditional financial intuitions partnered with CEXs to offer 'crypto debit cards', enabling users to pay merchants with their cryptocurrency holdings by converting them to fiat currencies at points of sale (POS). Several organizations have also started selling their goods and services for payments in cryptocurrencies through tailor-made DApps. For instance, in 2021, AXA Insurance in Switzerland started accepting Bitcoin as payment for all its non-life insurance products.

The DeFi landscape, although rapidly expanding, is still in its nascent stages, which means several risks around it need yet to be weeded out. Smart contract vulnerabilities, platform insolvencies, and the lack of legal frameworks can pose significant threats to users' assets. Furthermore, the volatile nature of cryptocurrencies, which are the primary mediums of exchange in DeFi platforms, can lead to significant uncertainties in transactions.

Regulation, or lack thereof, remains a contentious topic within the DeFi community. There's growing consensus that some form of regulation will be beneficial to this space. This will protect users from fraudulent schemes and ensure stability and longevity of the ecosystem. An ideal regulatory framework for DeFi would involve clear guidelines that protect user interests without stifling innovation. It would recognize the unique attributes of DeFi platforms and provide a balance between oversight and autonomy. As the ecosystem matures, collaboration between DeFi developers, users, and regulators will be crucial to ensure that the industry can thrive without compromising the principles that make it revolutionary.

It's becoming increasingly evident that DeFi has the potential to reDeFine (no pun intended) our understanding of finance, and that its journey to mass adoption ahead requires careful navigation, balancing innovation with prudence. It might only be a matter of time before you see your local bank branch manager at a government sponsored DeFi-orientation conference!

28.

ASSET TOKENIZATION: BENEFITS AND CHALLENGES

In chapter 12, we discussed cryptocurrency tokens, and how they have various types of utilities in blockchain-based project ecosystems. Can one of these utilities be to signify ownership of real-world assets? Well, yes it can. And although that's the concept behind non-fungible tokens (NFTs), even fungible tokens can be designed to represent real-world assets.

'Asset tokenization' is the process of converting ownership rights of real-world assets into cryptocurrency tokens (fungible or non-fungible).

We saw how this works with NFTs in chapter 21, where an NFT's metadata holds the identifying characteristics of the asset it represents, and the NFT itself signifies ownership of the asset. With fungible tokens, this process works in a similar way, where the token's smart contract has the identifying characteristics of an asset written into it, and each token minted by the smart contract gives the holder a certain percentage ownership of the asset.

Asset tokenization opens up a myriad of opportunities for the DeFi ecosystem at large, by enabling novel decentralized ownership mechanisms of illiquid assets, democratizing investment opportunities, and providing indisputable proof of asset ownership which is beneficial for owners and investors alike.

The most lauded benefit of asset tokenization is liquidity. Tokenization can make buying and selling very convenient and fast for assets that are traditionally illiquid (or, arduous to buy and sell), such as real estate and art. This not only broadens the market for these assets but also potentially increases their value due to their newfound liquidity.

Asset tokenization also democratizes investment opportunities. By breaking down assets into smaller digital units, tokenization makes it feasible for smaller investors to own a piece of assets that would otherwise be out of reach, such as rare antiquities and high-value artwork. This accessibility fosters inclusivity and diversity within investment portfolios.

Here's an example how this might work. Imagine if France decides to divide up the ownership of the Mona Lisa through tokenization. Each token would then represent a percentage of ownership of the famous painting, say 0.0001%, and 1,000,000 tokens could be made available at a price of, say 10,000$ each. This would put the value of the painting at a whopping 10 billion$ but allow smaller investors to truly own a share of the painting. This ownership could be passive, or the investors could collectively be allowed to actively participate in decisions regarding the curation of the painting through a DAO mechanism of token-gated voting. That isn't a recommendation to the French government, I'm just saying it would be cool if it happens!

Blockchain technology's inherent attributes, including immutability and transparency, ensure that the ownership and transaction history of any tokenized asset is reliably recorded and easily verifiable. This transparency reduces the potential for fraud and simplifies the due diligence process for asset buyers and sellers alike.

However, as exciting as all this sounds, the concept of asset tokenization has significant challenges to overcome before it is adopted at any noticeable scale.

Regulatory compliance is a prominent hurdle. Tokenization, which often deals with physical assets, must navigate a complex web of international laws and regulations. Regulatory and legal ambiguity around asset ownership mechanisms can deter adoption due to uncertainty for those involved in the tokenization of assets.

Another challenge is the need for a robust technological infrastructure that can support the reliability of asset tokenization mechanisms. The creation, issuance, and management of digital tokens require sophisticated systems that are completely fool-proof, secure, scalable, and interoperable with different blockchain platforms and traditional financial systems. For instance, you wouldn't want to lose your apartment if you lose the 12-word seed phrase to your blockchain account!

Lastly, while the idea of increased liquidity is appealing, market volatility poses risks. The ease of trading tokenized assets might lead to rapid fluctuations in their prices, which in turn could create uncertainties around their perceived value and erode investor confidence. Moreover, it doesn't help that prices of tokenized assets (especially those traded on DEXs) are often underpinned by other cryptocurrencies, which are very volatile themselves.

The broader DeFi ecosystem, at the moment, is nowhere close to solving all these challenges standing in the way of asset tokenization at scale. Which is to say, it might be a while before you can own a piece of Mona Lisa!

PHEW!

29.

VULNERABILITIES AND SECURITY MEASURES FOR CRYPTOCURRENCIES

The emergence of cryptocurrencies as a new asset class has revolutionized the financial landscape, offering a decentralized approach to investments and transactions. However, this innovation, like any other in the financial world, is not without vulnerabilities.

While blockchain technology promises immutable and secure elements, the interfaces and human factors introduce a spectrum of risks, such as scams, hacks and thefts that affect both custodial and non-custodial cryptocurrency holders. Let's look at some common ways in which cryptocurrency investments can be compromised, and the security measures that have been designed and rolled out to mitigate the risks.

Rugpulls are a form of exit scam where developers abandon a project and flee with investors' funds that are typically in liquidity pools (LPs), which drives the underlying token's price to zero immediately and dramatically. **These** present a significant risk primarily to non-custodial investors buying niche tokens. A notorious example is the Meerkat Finance rugpull of 2021, where developers absconded with 31 million$ by altering smart contract permissions. A notable defense against such scams is thorough due diligence on new projects and initial coin offerings (ICOs), including team transparency, smart contract code audits by reputable firms, and tracking the liquidity provisions' history.

Honeypots are malicious smart contract traps where tokens can be purchased but not sold, except by a few select addresses that belong to the creators. These schemes, like rugpulls, also prey upon non-custodial investors buying niche tokens. An investor buying such tokens will find themselves unable to sell, effectively losing their investment. While specific examples are less publicized, numerous small-scale honeypot scams have been reported, particularly in the realm of ICOs and new token launches. These can be mitigated by scrutinizing the smart contract's code to ensure it has both buying and selling functions or using trusted decentralized exchanges (DEXs) with a strong track record.

Dusting attacks are subtle, malicious maneuvers where attackers distribute small amounts of a cryptocurrency ('dust') to multiple addresses. This tactic, also targeted at non-custodial cryptocurrency holders, aims to compromise the privacy of wallet holders by linking the dusted coins to the recipients' other transactions and thereby identifying them for future phishing attacks or other forms of cyber exploitation. In late 2018 and early 2019, dusting attacks specifically targeted the Bitcoin and Litecoin communities, exploiting transaction public records to breach user privacy. The primary defense against dusting attacks involves the vigilant monitoring of unexpected, minuscule deposits in wallets and employing enhanced privacy measures, such as using new addresses for each transaction and leveraging privacy-focused coins or wallets.

Malicious smart contracts can be coded to execute unauthorized actions, such as spending or transferring cryptocurrencies without consent. These pose threats to non-custodial investors who interact directly with these contracts. There have been several instances of malicious smart contracts linked to legitimate-looking DApps offering lucrative opportunities such as high-yield lotteries but designed to drain the blockchain accounts that connect to them. Utilizing platforms that employ rigorous smart contract auditing services and engaging in community discourse can serve as a safeguard.

While malicious smart contracts are intentional, **code vulnerabilities in smart contracts are often unintended errors that can be exploited**. The Parity Wallet hack of 2017, which resulted in a loss of 30 million$, was due to a bug in the wallet's smart contract. Another example is the DAO hack of 2016, where Ether coins worth 50 million$ were stolen by attackers exploiting a smart contract vulnerability which allowed them to make multiple withdrawals in a single transaction. Frequent and rigorous smart contract security audits and ongoing bug bounty programs can mitigate these risks.

Hacks and systemic failures of centralized exchanges (CEXs) represent significant vulnerabilities for custodial holdings. The Mt. Gox hack of 2014, where 480 million$ worth of Bitcoin was stolen, remains a sobering milestone in crypto history. More recently, another large CEX called FTX underwent a systemic failure due to mismanagement of user funds, resulting in losses of ~8 billion$. Regulatory oversight is constantly evolving to create robust guard-rails around CEX operations to mitigate these risks. For instance, regulations imposing measures such as 2-factor authentication, cold storage for majority of assets held, mandatory and frequent proof-of-funds reports, and insured custodial services have become commonplace in many financial jurisdictions.

And lastly, both custodial and non-custodial users can fall victim to **phishing attacks, where they are deceived into revealing private keys or sending funds to scammers.** The Electrum Wallet Phishing scam in 2018 cost users millions. Vigilance, using hardware 2-factor authentication devices, and never sharing seed phrases are key preventive measures against these types of attacks.

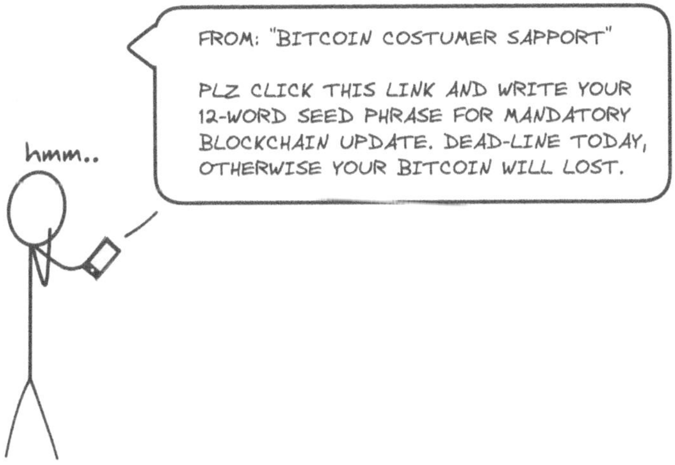

The industry has not been idle in responding to these vulnerabilities. The ever-evolving technological response involves the development of more secure protocols akin to those in traditional finance. For instance, CEX applications come with advanced security features such as 2-factor authentication. Smart contracts can be embedded with safety checks that prevent fund transfer unless certain specific conditions are met. For instance, multi-signature ('multisig') smart contracts require multiple keys to authorize a transaction, much like requiring several officers to launch a nuclear missile, a safeguard against unilateral, unauthorized actions.

The regulatory climate has also been maturing to create clarity around rules for how cryptocurrencies and related businesses can operate. Slowly but surely, the world is marching towards more uniform regulations that are easy to understand and navigate by the industry, and are aimed towards protecting users from vulnerabilities.

With each technological and regulatory advancement in the right direction, the industry inches closer to a perfect balance where the freedom of decentralization doesn't come at the cost of security.

30.

ADDRESSING MISINFORMATION IN THE CRYPTO-SPACE

Misinformation in the crypto space often exploits the complexity and novelty of blockchain technology. For many, the technical jargon and rapidly evolving landscape can be overwhelming, making it difficult to distinguish between legitimate opportunities and scams. Fraudsters capitalize on this confusion, crafting sophisticated schemes that can be hard to spot at times even for cautious eyes. Examples abound, from phishing attacks to fake initial coin offerings (ICOs) and from rugpulls to honeypots, each designed to exploit the trust and curiosity of unsuspecting individuals.

Social media platforms like Telegram and Discord, popular among crypto communities for their privacy and direct communication features, have become hotbeds for scams. Telegram, with its encrypted messaging, hosts numerous 'pump and dump' groups where scammers artificially inflate the price of obscure cryptocurrencies only to sell off their holdings at a peak, leaving other investors with worthless assets. Discord servers, though initially designed for gamers, now host a plethora of crypto trading rooms where misinformation about the next 'big cryptocurrency' can spread like wildfire, trapping those looking for a quick profit in schemes too good to be true.

Misinformation has, at times, even proliferated on mainstream platforms such as X (formerly Twitter) and YouTube. Fraudulent actors have even exploited deepfake technology to create highly convincing videos on these platforms. These videos often appear to show celebrities endorsing questionable cryptocurrencies or promoting schemes that promise instant returns. In many such recent incidents, unsuspecting individuals were enticed to 'invest' their cryptocurrency holdings with the assurance of receiving an instant double return, leveraging the trust and appeal of well-known personalities to lend credibility to these deceptive offers.

The decentralized nature of cryptocurrencies means there is no central authority to verify the information being disseminated. This decentralization, while protecting users from censorship and control by any single entity, also means there is no centralized mechanism for addressing misinformation. The burden of due diligence, therefore, falls heavily on the individual investor. In a space where pseudonymity is celebrated and transactions are irreversible, the consequences of falling for a scam can be devastating, with no recourse for recovery.

Moreover, the proliferation of misinformation has broader implications for the crypto space. It not only affects individual investors but also undermines the credibility and stability of the market. When fear, uncertainty, and doubt (FUD) are spread deliberately, it can lead to market volatility, with prices swinging wildly based on rumours rather than fundamentals. This environment of mistrust makes it challenging for legitimate projects to gain the recognition they deserve, slowing the overall progress of blockchain technology.

Addressing misinformation in the crypto space, therefore, requires a multi-faceted approach. Education is key. By increasing awareness and understanding of blockchain technology, individuals can be better equipped to navigate these waters safely. Initiatives by crypto communities, industry leaders, and even regulators to provide clear, accessible information can help demystify the technology and empower users to make informed decisions.

Moreover, while decentralization poses challenges for regulating misinformation, it also offers solutions. Blockchain technology itself can be leveraged to create more transparent, secure, and immutable systems for information sharing and verification, thus mitigating the risks posed by its own decentralized nature. Additionally, there are a number of specialized projects that provide automated fact-checking and smart contract auditing services, which can contribute significantly to a more trustworthy ecosystem.

Ultimately, combating misinformation in the crypto space is a collective effort that requires vigilance, education, and innovation. As the technology evolves, so too will the strategies for spreading and fighting misinformation. By fostering a culture of controlled scepticism and due diligence, alongside developing tools and systems for verification, the crypto community can navigate the challenges of its decentralized landscape, protecting itself from the scams and misinformation that threaten its integrity.

31.

THE REGULATORY LANDSCAPE OF CRYPTOCURRENCIES

The word 'regulation' has come up in almost every chapter so far, as if it is a magic wand for disappearing all issues faced by blockchain technology and cryptocurrencies. While reality might not be as simple or as dramatic, regulation does have a pivotal part to play in shaping the future of this landscape.

Regulation encompasses the rules and standards set by governing bodies or authorized institutions to maintain order and integrity, and safeguard consumer interests. In the financial sector, regulation is vital for mitigating systemic risks, preventing financial crimes such as fraud and money laundering, and protecting investors from market manipulation and unfair business practices.

The topic of regulating blockchain technology, especially cryptocurrencies, has been contentious. While many people advocate leaving this space alone and immune to regulation in the spirit of true decentralization, others push for balanced regulation to foster innovation while ensuring market integrity, consumer protection, and financial stability in the face of technologies that challenge traditional financial paradigms.

Effective regulation of cryptocurrencies requires a nuanced understanding of blockchain technology and international cooperation to address the borderless nature of digital assets. This involves establishing clear guidelines for the classification and treatment of cryptocurrencies, enhancing cybersecurity measures to enable secure decentralization, and promoting transparency and accountability while preserving confidentiality of sensitive user and business data.

As such, the regulatory responses to cryptocurrencies vary significantly across the globe at the moment, reflecting widely differing national priorities and perspectives on innovation, consumer protection, and financial security. While countries like El Salvador openly embrace cryptocurrencies by recognizing Bitcoin as legal tender, some others like China have historically issued outright bans on any activities concerning cryptocurrencies.

Between these polar opposites, there are jurisdictions that take more balanced regulatory stances. For instance, the European Union is moving towards a harmonized approach with its proposed "Markets in Crypto-Assets" (MiCA) regulations, aiming for a unified framework that encourages innovation while protecting investors.

There are some common regulatory themes that stand out across global jurisdictions. For instance, the increasing recognition of the potential for cryptocurrencies to be used in money laundering and financing illegal activities has necessitated the implementation of anti-money laundering (AML) and know your customer

(KYC) standards. AML standards scrutinize financial transactions to prevent the laundering of illicitly obtained funds, while KYC processes require the identification and verification of clients' identities.

Emerging technologies, such as blockchain analytics tools and zero-knowledge proofs (ZKPs), offer promising avenues for reconciling the need for AML/KYC compliance with the inherent benefits of blockchain technology, such as privacy and decentralization. These technologies enable the monitoring of transactions for suspicious activities while preserving pseudonymity, representing a step towards innovative solutions that respect the core principles of cryptocurrencies.

Another common regulatory theme that is often fiercely debated is how cryptocurrencies should be taxed, and if excessively doing so stifles innovation by restricting user and developer interest in blockchain technology as a whole. We'll cover these aspects in the next chapter.

As the world grapples with the meteoric rise of the popularity of cryptocurrencies, the development of coherent, comprehensive and forward-looking regulatory frameworks will be crucial. These frameworks must be adaptable to keep up with technological advancements and emerging market realities, fostering an environment that promotes financial inclusion, safeguards public interests, and leverages the transformative potential of cryptocurrencies for global economic development.

32.

TAX-IMPLICATONS OF CRYPTOCURRENCY INVESTMENTS

Cryptocurrencies offer novel and innovative investment opportunities and new avenues for financial transactions. This implies that they are on the tax-man's radar, like any other asset class or transaction avenue. They come with a host of complex tax implications that individuals and businesses often grapple with.

Tax regulations globally are rapidly evolving to include cryptocurrencies within their frameworks, through capital gains taxes, income taxes, and sales taxes. We'll briefly cover the essence of these three types of taxes here, but keep in mind that these are high-level descriptions which are not specific to any jurisdictions' tax regulations, and therefore should not be directly used as tactical guidelines for tax calculations in any way.

Capital gains taxes are levied on profits realized through cryptocurrency investments. The sale or exchange of cryptocurrencies, resulting in profit, is generally considered a taxable event, similar to the tax treatment of traditional investments like stocks or real estate. However, the volatile nature of cryptocurrencies, and their trade across various centralized and decentralized exchanges (CEXs and DEXs) often pose challenges in calculating capital gains accurately. Further, different global jurisdictions often issue different (and ever-changing) accounting guidelines to calculate capital gains from cryptocurrencies, making it difficult to develop standardized and automated solutions to do the calculations for investors.

Income taxes are levied on cryptocurrency earnings through various activities. In many jurisdictions' tax regulations, receiving cryptocurrencies as payments or through mining or staking necessitates reporting their fair market value as taxable income.

Lastly, **sales taxes are levied on cryptocurrencies used in transactions involving goods and services.** For instance, if you use cryptocurrency to buy a laptop, the value of the cryptocurrency at the time of the purchase needs to be reported for tax purposes, as if you had provided goods or services of equal value in exchange for the laptop.

Pseudonymity of non-custodial cryptocurrency holdings does not extend to tax implications. Tax authorities are becoming increasingly adept at using blockchain analysis tools and international cooperation to track, trace, and tax cryptocurrency transactions. For instance, CEXs often function under regulations like traditional financial institutions, reporting large transactions to authorities. In some jurisdictions, they also report cryptocurrency withdrawals along with the recipient blockchain account addresses, which essentially kills their pseudonymity.

On the other hand, several countries have adopted a crypto-friendly stance, offering tax exemptions or lenient policies in attempts to attract investments and become hubs of blockchain innovation. This contrasts with countries imposing stringent reporting requirements, where non-disclosure of cryptocurrency holdings or gains can result in severe penalties.

The regulatory landscape for cryptocurrencies is continually shifting, leading to changes in taxation laws and practices. Governments are working towards clearer guidelines and regulations, including distinguishing between different types of tokens, each carrying unique tax implications. The exploration of central bank digital currencies (CBDCs) by some countries could further reshape the taxation landscape for digital currencies.

NEW FRONTIERS AND FUTURE OUTLOOK

33.

ORDINALS: A NEW TYPE OF NON-FUNGIBILITY

The Bitcoin blockchain, traditionally known for its robustness in handling financial transactions, did not inherently support the creation of non-fungible tokens (NFTs). Though layer-2 networks on top the Bitcoin blockchain such as Counterparty and Stacks do have NFTs, these are still outside the main Bitcoin blockchain.

Since its inception, Bitcoin has allowed for the embedding of non-transaction data, such as text messages, within its blocks. In fact, Satoshi Nakamoto himself included a message in Bitcoin's genesis block – "The Times 03/Jan/2009 Chancellor on brink of second bailout for banks". Updates to the Bitcoin protocol such as SegWit in 2017 and Taproot in 2021 brought along advancements in this regard, which significantly increased the amount of data (including these types of messages) that can be embedded into blocks.

In January 2023, developer-artist Casey Rodarmor introduced **the 'ordinals' theory, which distinctly numbers individual Satoshis in their order of creation**

in the entire timeline of the Bitcoin blockchain. Satoshis, as you know, are the lowest denomination of Bitcoins, with one Bitcoin being made of 100 million Satoshis. As per the ordinals theory, the first Satoshi from the block rewards of the genesis block is Satoshi #1, and the count goes up from there.

At the same time, Rodarmor also introduced the concept of **'inscription', which means writing data on individual Satoshis.** This is an innovative concept made possible by advancements that happened through the SegWit and Taproot updates to the Bitcoin protocol. The 'inscribed' data on Satoshis can be of various types and formats, such as text and images. So now, messages can be written not only on Bitcoin blocks, but also inscribed on individual Satoshis with this innovation.

The ordinal theory and inscriptions together introduced an inventive method for creating NFT-like assets, which came to be simply called 'ordinals'. In contrast to traditional NFTs, which rely on smart contracts on specialized blockchains like Ethereum, this method inscribes the unique identifying data of assets directly onto Satoshis. This effectively transforms each numbered and inscribed Satoshi into a unique non-fungible asset, or an ordinal.

To better understand the concept of ordinals, consider this analogy: Picture all the 1$ bills in circulation, each having the same value but a unique serial number. Now, imagine an artist adds a doodle to one of these 1$ bills. Identified by its distinct serial number, this particular bill becomes more than just a currency note, it's now a unique piece of art, potentially accruing value and becoming a collector's item, especially if the artist is renowned.

Now replace 1$ bills with Satoshis, serial numbers with ordinal numbers, and the artist's doodle with a digital inscription. This is, in essence, how ordinals work, turning each numbered and inscribed Satoshi into a distinct and potentially valuable digital asset, with its underlying value coming from the perception of the data inscribed on it.

Ordinals, which are basically numbered and inscribed Satoshis, can be systematically transacted on Taproot-compatible Bitcoin wallets. These wallets are specially designed to use a first-in-first-out (FIFO) mechanism for transacting Satoshis, which means amongst all available Satoshis in a Bitcoin address, the first one to leave during a transaction is the first one that entered it. Leveraging this FIFO rule, these wallets help to specifically target and route ordinals. For instance, ordinal Satoshis won't be simply given away as part of gas fees.

Ordinals on the Bitcoin network embed entire digital assets directly onto Satoshis, rather than relying on external links for storage like traditional NFTs do. This integration ensures that the assets inherit Bitcoin's security, immutability, and decentralization, offering a level of permanence and independence from third-party platforms. This method results in a more secure and enduring representation of digital assets, fully ingrained in the blockchain's architecture.

The ordinals system also introduces another dimension of rarity and collectability within the Bitcoin network. Based on the the history of the blocks in which they were created, individual numbered but un-inscribed (blank) Satoshis themselves are classified into various categories, ranging from common to mythic. This has opened up even more opportunities for collectors and enthusiasts in the cryptocurrency space, allowing for the trading of unique Satoshis based on their history within the secure and robust framework of the Bitcoin blockchain.

However the introduction of ordinals has been very controversial, to say the least. Most critics argue that this new application diverts from Bitcoin's original purpose as a digital currency and could lead to increased competition for block space due to all the additional data being added, potentially resulting in higher transaction fees. These concerns have sparked debates within the Bitcoin community about the future direction and scalability of the network.

The Bitcoin protocol, in essence, does not formally recognize the numbering of Satoshis or any inscriptions on them, in the same way as a central bank will not formally recognize a doodled 1$ bill. Rather, a community of passionate ordinal enthusiasts led by Rodarmor has come together to collectively recognize this system and build tools to support it. Which essentially means, ordinals can still be normally transacted as ordinary Satoshis ignoring the numberings and inscriptions. Indeed, many fungibility advocates within the Bitcoin community don't acknowledge the existence of ordinals at all. This is one more way in which ordinals are markedly different from traditional NFTs, for instance an NFT on the Ethereum blockchain cannot be ignored or transacted as an Ether coin.

Nonetheless, ordinals gained considerable traction in 2023. Within a span of a few months, other blockchains have also adopted the ordinals system, simply because it is cheaper to send around inscribed denominations of cryptocurrencies between addresses than to pay the relatively higher gas fees to run smart contracts of NFT collections. But this has also, ironically, raised overall gas prices due to the increased competition for block space.

Where this system goes in the future is a matter of speculation at this point. What we do know for sure, is if Alice and Bob exchange their Bitcoins one-for-one, they might not end up with the same thing after all.

34.

BLOCKCHAIN AND METAVERSE

The metaverse refers to a vast collection of virtual environments that simulate real-life experiences, where users can work, play, and interact in general. From being just a fictional idea that was the subject of movies like 'The Matrix', 'Tron', and 'Inception', it is gradually on its way to becoming a part of our everyday reality.

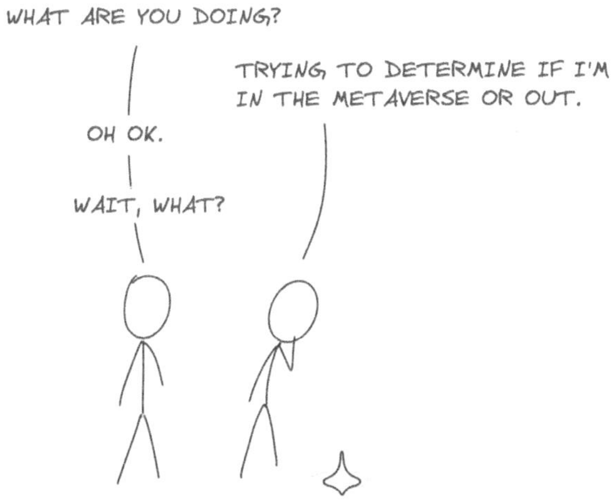

One of the earliest implementations of the metaverse which aligns with our current interpretations of the concept was a multimedia platform called 'Second Life' that came out in 2003, where people could create characters (avatars) for themselves and interact with other users. Since then, the technology has come a long way, and today there are entire virtual worlds like 'Decentraland', 'The Sandbox' and 'Roblox', which allow users to create, experience, and monetize content and applications. It has also evolved beyond PC-based interfaces like in 'Second Life' and now incorporates advanced experiential technologies, such as Virtual Reality (VR) and Augmented Reality (AR), greatly enhancing the overall user experience.

In this expansive digital realm, blockchain technology has already emerged a pivotal player, shaping its structure and functionality. Blockchain's role in the metaverse is multifaceted, addressing critical aspects of asset/content ownership, identity, and economics.

Through innovations such as non-fungible tokens (NFTs), blockchain technology introduces a paradigm shift in how virtual assets are owned and managed. NFTs have become a prominent way of owning digital assets in many metaverse platforms. For instance, in Decentraland and The Sandbox users can own, buy, and sell land and other assets as NFTs.

In the economic landscape of the metaverse, blockchain technology facilitates transactions and underpins the economic systems within these virtual spaces. Cryptocurrencies have become currencies of the metaverse, allowing users to conduct transactions, buy virtual goods, and even earn income through activities like play-to-earn (P2E) gaming. For instance, in 'Axie Infinity', a blockchain-based game, players can earn crypto tokens called 'Axie Infinity Shards' through gameplay, which can be traded on various centralized and decentralized cryptocurrency exchanges (CEXs and DEXs).

Looking ahead, the metaverse, bolstered by blockchain technology, holds immense potential to evolve further. It's poised to become a hub for a wide array of activities including education, professional development, art, and entertainment.

Blockchain's role in this future of the metaverse will likely extend to areas such as enabling decentralized governance in it, and seamlessly integrating (augmenting) real-world elements into it. Blockchain technology and its innovations such as smart contracts could support community-led governance models in the metaverse, empowering users to collectively create and enforce rules without central oversight. Additionally, blockchain's secure data handling capabilities could be effectively leveraged for safely incorporating large amounts of real-time physical-world data into the Metaverse (e.g., through the internet of things which we will talk about in the next chapter), enhancing virtual environment experiences.

But, like the potential, the challenges ahead are also substantial. Issues such as scalability, interoperability, and user privacy need to be addressed to fully realize this vision. As the metaverse evolves, blockchain technology will need to adapt and grow, ensuring that this digital universe remains secure, efficient, and accessible.

The integration of blockchain technology with the metaverse is paving the way for innovative digital interactions and a new digital economy. This collaboration signifies a future where digital and physical realms are more interconnected, enhancing the authenticity and impact of virtual experiences. As we delve deeper into this integration, it will progressively redefine the boundaries between our digital and physical worlds, offering novel possibilities and challenges that we are just starting to explore.

35.

BLOCKCHAIN AND IOT

The internet of things (IoT) refers to networks of physical objects that are embedded with sensors, software, and other technologies for the purpose of collecting and/or exchanging data. A common example of an IoT application is a smart home that you interact with by saying things like "Alexa, turn on kitchen lights", or "Siri, play some music on living room stereo".

IoT is an up-and-coming technology that is being increasingly leveraged across several applications, from small scale smart homes to very large scale smart cities. The networks of physical objects in these applications are capable of handling data in various ways, including collecting, processing, storing and transmitting it.

That's where blockchain technology comes in. IoT's vast networks of interconnected devices could be transformed by blockchain's decentralized and secure ledgers, addressing many of its existing challenges notably in security, scalability, and automation.

Blockchains' cryptographic security could fortify IoT networks, safeguarding them against potential breaches. Blockchains could ensure the integrity of data flowing between the myriad of IoT-connected devices, creating immutable records of transactions and exchanges. Private blockchains could be used if the exchanges need to be confidential. This would not only enhance trust in IoT systems but would also guarantee data accuracy and security, essential in sectors like healthcare and defence.

Blockchain technology also holds potential for addressing scalability challenges in IoT. As IoT networks expand with more connected devices, the demand for a robust system to manage the increasing data influx becomes crucial. Blockchain technology offers a promising way to manage this data seamlessly and securely, thereby enhancing the scalability of IoT systems. Take smart cities, for instance. Through blockchain, intricate and vast networks involved in public services within a smart city, ranging from traffic control to energy distribution, could be managed more efficiently and transparently. For instance, sensors in public transport could optimize routes and schedules in real-time, recorded on blockchains for reliability and coordination. This would ensure not only efficiency but also the reliability and integrity of the data critical for smooth functioning of smart cities.

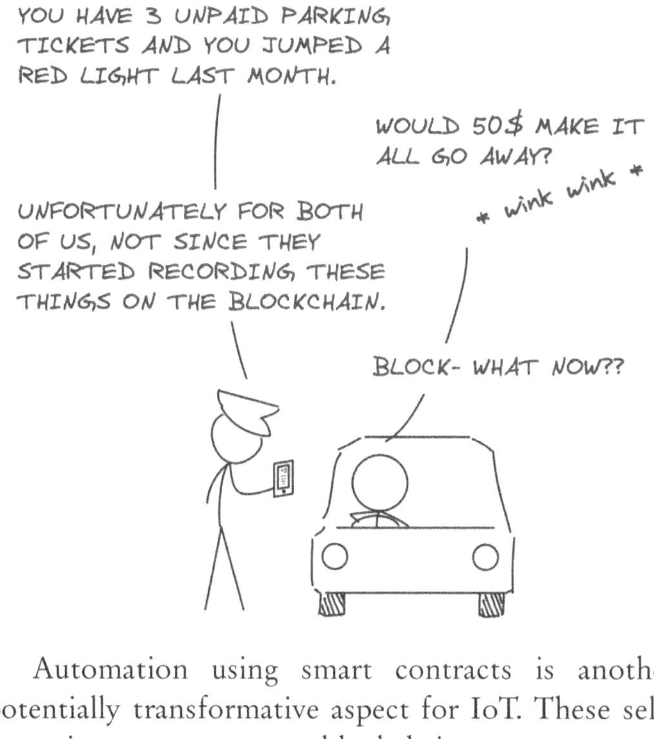

Automation using smart contracts is another potentially transformative aspect for IoT. These self-executing contracts on blockchains can automate interactions within IoT ecosystems. Functions in smart contracts could be programmed to both send and receive data to and from IoT devices. Remember the example from chapter 7 about Alice renting Bob's apartment? Imagine if the smart contract from that was connected to a digital door-lock on the apartment that would be automatically coded to Alice's fingerprints once her payment is completed.

In turn, blockchain technology could benefit from the real-time data collected by IoT networks, which opens the door for several interesting applications. For instance, blockchains for supply chain management can rely on IoT devices to automatically provide tracking data of goods from origin to consumer, which can reduce human errors. In healthcare, private blockchains can enable the secure storage of patient data from remote IoT devices, with smart contracts automatically analyzing this data to trigger necessary medical interventions or dispensations.

The possibilities with this symbiotic integration are rich. The convergence of IoT and blockchain is a paradigm shift towards a more automated, secure, and efficient world, where digital and physical realities merge seamlessly, unlocking innovative frontiers in industrial operations as well as day-to-day life. However such integration is not without challenges. Regulatory hurdles, technological advancements to address issues like blockchain's energy consumption, and ensuring data privacy in an increasingly interconnected world are key areas that need addressing to extract its full potential.

36.

BLOCKCHAIN AND AI

Artificial intelligence (AI), in a nutshell, is the science of building machines that can perform tasks requiring human intelligence such as perception, problem-solving, and decision-making. It is among the most significant technological advancements of our time, and unless you are living under a rock, you'd have heard about it and probably even used it already

As ground-breaking as it is, AI has lately sparked a lot of debate critically examining issues around it, such as quality and availability of data used to train AI models, inherent biases in AI algorithms, and potential risks associated with ethically questionable actions and decisions made by AI.

Blockchain technology's decentralized and immutable data handling capabilities could potentially make AI more equitable and trustworthy, alleviating some of these issues.

A key benefit blockchain technology could bring to AI is the democratization of data access for its development. Currently, large corporations own a lot of data crucial for development of certain types of AI models, limiting wider innovation. For instance, social networks own vast user behavior data, essential for training AI models predicting user mindsets and needs in various contexts. Blockchain technology's decentralized frameworks could change this dynamic. In a decentralized social network, most user data would be recorded on distributed ledgers, making it accessible to wider audiences. This would allow smaller companies and even individual researchers to access vital data, fostering diverse and creative AI solutions. In essence, blockchain could level the playing field in AI development by ensuring equitable data access.

Blockchain technology also holds potential to enhance the trustworthiness of AI by demystifying its often perceived 'black box' nature in decision-making. By recording AI actions on blockchains, each decision would be transparently and traceably logged, ensuring accountability and allowing for audits. This is especially crucial in sectors like healthcare, law, and defence, where the outcomes of AI decisions are critical. For instance, a blockchain-logged AI model analysing patient data to recommend treatment plans would be less of a black box to healthcare professionals, who would be able to review the exact data points, algorithms and decisions that the model made. Such a system would not only build trust among users and regulatory bodies but also ensure that AI decisions are fair, ethically sound, and aligned with human values.

In turn, the various kinds of AI models and capabilities that are under development have the potential to enhance user-friendliness, security, and efficiency of blockchain networks and applications.

In enhancing transaction security and fraud detection, AI's advanced pattern recognition algorithms could be adapted to decentralized finance (DeFi), much like their application in conventional finance. These algorithms are adept at discerning intricate transaction patterns and could play a crucial role in thwarting unauthorized activities within blockchain networks. AI's ability to detect irregularities could also extend to smart contracts, to spot potentially malicious content and alert users, thereby safeguarding their interactions within the blockchain ecosystem.

AI's natural language processing capabilities could streamline the development of smart contracts, reducing errors and making them more secure. AI could also be used to facilitate the creation of more advanced and intuitive decentralized applications (DApps). For instance, AI models could be trained by leveraging historical wallet-interaction data to predict user preferences and adapt their user interfaces accordingly, which would significantly improve user experience.

While the potential of these ideas is significant, it faces challenges such as blockchain scalability and the energy consumption of AI systems. Ongoing innovations like layer-2 blockchain solutions and more energy-efficient AI algorithms show promise in overcoming these hurdles, and we could see the synergies between the two technologies play out soon.

The association of AI and blockchain is about more than just technological advancement, it represents a move towards a more connected, transparent, and equitable digital world. It holds immense potential to reshape industries, create fair and efficient intelligent systems, and pioneer new technology frontiers. This journey towards an AI and blockchain-integrated future exemplifies the boundless possibilities of technological collaboration and innovation.

37.

THE LONG TERM VISION OF A DECENTRALIZED WORLD

A decentralized world would be one that leverages blockchain technology's core premise of decentralization to fully transform various facets of society. If/how/when this fully plays out is anyone's guess as of now, but it's still exciting to think about. Perhaps blockchain technology will spread its wings over society to make it fully decentralized, or maybe another similar innovation will replace it, offering all its benefits and more – who knows?

Nonetheless, a good place to conclude this book would be to speculate a bit, about what such a world driven by blockchain technology would look like. Let's specifically look at what this would mean for some of the most significant facets of society: finances, social interactions, and governance.

The effect of blockchain technology has already begun to unsettle the bedrock of traditional financial systems through the surge of cryptocurrencies and the emergence of decentralized finance (DeFi). In the future, this landscape could undergo an even more radical shift.

Imagine a world where traditional banking is completely transformed by the integration of blockchain technology. In this world, all transactions happen on seamlessly bridged blockchains, and every 'bank account' is a blockchain account activated through an on-chain know your customer (KYC) process. These blockchain accounts are the hubs for all your financial activities, including making day-to-day transactions, investments, and even receiving your monthly salary in the cryptocurrency of your choice.

The KYC process to open accounts is entirely on-chain leveraging innovations such as zero-knowledge proofs (ZKPs), prioritizing user privacy and data security. Unlike traditional systems where institutions have access to user data, here individuals store their data on secure, decentralized networks, and use ZKPs to share it privately and selectively for KYC verification.

Security in this new financial landscape is paramount. Private keys to blockchain accounts are secured using biometric encryption, not just mnemonically as seed phrases. No biometric data is stored on any centralized databases, though. For instance, imagine an algorithm that encrypts your seed phrase with the unique pattern of your retina as the key. This way, no image of your retina gets stored anywhere, and access to your account requires your physical presence.

Such approaches could also be complemented by other blockchain-based security measures. For instance, high-value cryptocurrency transactions could require additional biometric authentication, adding yet another extra layer of security and user control.

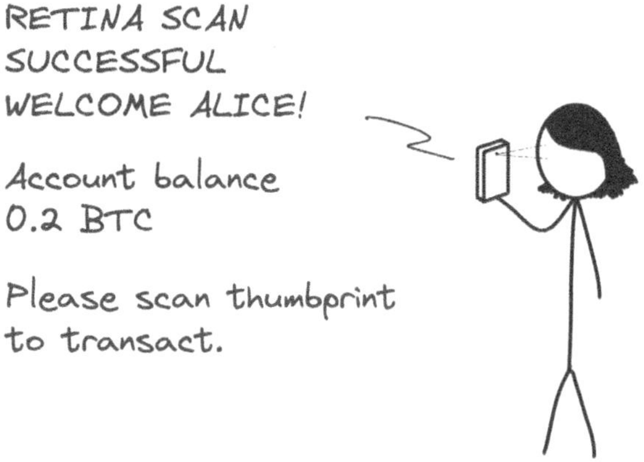

In chapter 26, we discussed that it's very unlikely for cryptocurrencies to ever replace fiat currencies completely, and they will play out as a blend of an asset class and an alternative currency. In this case, it is likely that major cryptocurrencies will become a popular and reliable asset class, and will be widely incorporated into national reserves alongside other assets such as major fiat currencies and gold.

But for a moment, imagine a world where a significant enough social revolution has happened, which has completely replaced fiat currencies with cryptocurrencies. Two salient features would define this world. One, cryptocurrencies become the natural standard for valuing goods and services. And two, given the inherently controlled supply of cryptocurrencies, this would mean a more stable inflation landscape compared to what we have at present with fiat currencies.

With decentralization, online social interaction could also be totally overhauled. Picture a world where social media platforms are entirely governed by their users, with blockchain technology empowering individuals to both collectively manage and financially benefit from these platforms. In this setup, users are not just content creators and consumers, they are also key decision-makers, directly involved in shaping platform algorithms and privacy policies.

Each social media platform also hosts its own marketplace, revolutionizing how creative work is distributed and monetized. Artists, writers, and creators can directly offer their content to audiences, bypassing traditional intermediaries. This direct-to-consumer approach ensures that creators receive equitable compensation for their work, in various cryptocurrencies. This system not only fosters a fairer economic model for creators but also strengthens the bond between creators and their audiences, as every interaction and transaction occurs without any intermediary and within the community-driven ecosystem of the platform.

With decentralization, a significant cultural shift towards community engagement and responsibility is necessitated. Decentralized networks, powered by blockchains, offer local communities the tools to autonomously manage and distribute their resources. This applies to aspects such as local energy distribution, public infrastructure development, culture and heritage preservation, environmental monitoring and protection, and several others. Such systems enhance the effectiveness of addressing local needs, driving a sense of collective responsibility and fostering innovation to develop tailored solutions to unique community-specific challenges.

This shift also applies to governance, where blockchain technology enables transparent and democratic decision-making processes. Communities can directly participate in influencing decisions that affect their lives, which not only makes governance more accountable but also bolsters societal resilience and cohesion.

Speaking of governance – in politics, as of now blockchain technology hasn't even begun to scratch the surface of its full potential. Blockchains' inherent transparency and security features promise more robust political mechanisms. Imagine a world where all voting happens on public blockchains, so it's completely transparent and immune to manipulation.

Additionally, in this world, governmental accountability is not just a mandate but an inbuilt feature of political processes. This is powered by blockchain technology – all manifestos, government finances and developmental projects are recorded on public blockchains.

Other than these facets of society, we are also bound to see similar transformation of several others. For instance, supply chains, travel and tourism, healthcare, insurance, real estate, and education could all be completely underpinned by blockchains, supported by innovations such as non-fungible tokens (NFTs), token-curated registries (TCRs), and ordinals. Imagine things like flight tickets, medicine prescriptions, apartment deeds and your child's homework on blockchains!

As cool as all this sounds, this vision would require significant advancements in blockchain technology, regulatory changes, and widespread societal adoption. Issues such as scalability, energy consumption, and the digital divide pose significant hurdles. As we integrate decentralized systems into our lives, the balance between innovation, ethical considerations, and sustainability becomes crucial.

The decentralized world we envision is one where efficiency, equity, and empowerment are not just ideals but everyday realities. It's a world that harnesses the power of blockchain technology to create a more inclusive, transparent, and accountable global society. As we stride into this future, it is essential to ensure that the transformative potential of decentralization is harnessed responsibly and equitably, shaping a world that benefits all.

WAIT, SO WHO ARE ALICE AND BOB?

Alice and Bob are fictional characters rooted in a tradition that spans several decades. They first made their appearance in a 1978 paper by Ron Rivest, Adi Shamir, and Leonard Adleman, who introduced RSA encryption, a cornerstone of internet security. In their scenario, Alice and Bob were used to explain how two parties could communicate securely over an insecure channel.

This initial portrayal captured the imagination of the cryptography and security community, leading Alice and Bob to become ubiquitous figures in academic papers and textbooks across disciplines, representing parties in countless theoretical scenarios. This book continues the tradition!

Oh, and in case you're wondering, Carol and Dave who made a small appearance with their sheep and vases, are alphabetical extensions of this fictional naming tradition – Alice, Bob, Carol, Dave.

YOUR FEEDBACK IS INVALUABLE!

While every possible effort has been made to ensure high quality and accuracy of this book's contents, spelling, grammar, and other errors might have crept in, particularly since this is the first edition of the author's first publication.

We appreciate you contacting the author first before taking any other actions on such errors, as this would enable quick fixes before they negatively impact the book.

Any other feedback would also be greatly appreciated, as it would go a long way to improve this book (and future ones by the author).

To share your thoughts or report errors, please reach out to the author at ajinkya.latkar@gmail.com.

Made in United States
Cleveland, OH
04 November 2026

47644440R00136